Village Trails

in

HAMPSHIRE

Village Walks
in
HAMPSHIRE

Anne-Marie Edwards

COUNTRYSIDE BOOKS
NEWBURY, BERKSHIRE

First published 1999
© Anne-Marie Edwards 1999
Reprinted 2002
Revised and updated 2006

COUNTRYSIDE BOOKS
3 Catherine Road
Newbury, Berkshire

ISBN 1 85306 560 9

Designed by Graham Whiteman
Photographs by Mike Edwards
Maps and illustrations by Trevor Yorke
Front cover photo shows South Street, Titchfield
Picture on page 3 shows the village of Martin

Produced through MRM Associates Ltd., Reading
Printed by J.W. Arrowsmith Ltd., Bristol

Contents

AREA MAP SHOWING THE LOCATION OF THE WALKS.

N

(11) Sherfield on Loddon

(9) Hurstbourne Tarrant (10) Hannington

BASINGSTOKE •

(12) Greywell

• ANDOVER

(8) Amport

(7) Wherwell

ALTON •

Alresford (13) Chawton (14)

(15) Selborne

WINCHESTER •

(16) Cheriton

(6) Mottisfont

PETERSFIELD •

(4) Martin

Breamore

(5)

Meonstoke (17)

(18) Burton

Fritham (3)

(2) Minstead

(19) Hambledon

• SOUTHAMPTON

FAREHAM

• RINGWOOD

(20)

• PORTSMOUTH

(1) Burley

Titchfield

For Chris and Paula Leigh

Publisher's Note

We hope that you obtain considerable enjoyment from this book; great care has been taken in its preparation. Although at the time of publication all routes followed public rights of way or permitted paths, diversion orders can be made and permissions withdrawn.

We cannot of course be held responsible for such diversion orders and any inaccuracies in the text which result from these or any other changes to the routes nor any damage which might result from walkers trespassing on private property. We are anxious though that all details covering the walks are kept up to date and would therefore welcome information from readers which would be relevant to future editions.

Introduction

Do you love old oak and beech woods, lush river valleys threaded by sparkling chalk streams, wide downland views and villages where time seems to have stood still? Then you will love walking in Hampshire. To these delights add a coast that has witnessed the greatest events in the Nation's history. Although best known for its two great ports, Southampton and Portsmouth, this attractive shore fringing the Solent for more than 70 miles is studded with ancient abbeys, forts and castles, lonely bird-haunted creeks and small harbours, and nature reserves exceptionally rich in wildlife.

In the west of the county is Hampshire's unique treasure, the still medieval landscape of the New Forest. Declared a royal hunting forest by William the Conqueror in 1079, this splendid area of rolling heaths and magnificent ancient woodlands extends for over 120 square miles. It is still the property of the Crown and by custom open for all to enjoy. Chalk hills form the heart of the county, rising in the north-west to create the beautiful uplands known as 'The Hampshire Highlands'. In the east the downs reach their highest southerly point at Butser Hill, a few miles north of Portsmouth.

Close to the Sussex border the chalk descends abruptly to the greensand rocks of the Weald, creating a truly dramatic landscape. These steep, densely-wooded hillsides known as hangers were immortalised by Gilbert White in his much-loved book *The Natural History and Antiquities of Selborne*. Jane Austen found the inspiration and setting for her later novels in the more gentle pastoral country further north around Alton. Hampshire's main rivers, the Avon, Test, Itchen and Meon, rise in the chalk to flow southwards carving wide valleys in the downs, peopled by man from earliest times and now sheltering some of the county's loveliest villages.

Although modern life has brought many changes, Hampshire villages have succeeded in retaining their old-world charm. Some villages, settled on the greensand rocks in the east, are built of local cream-coloured malmstone, but elsewhere, on chalk or clay, more homely materials had to be used. Many houses and cottages are timber-framed, the dark wood often contrasting with rich red brick infilling. Others may be built of cob or flint tucked beneath deep-eaved thatched roofs. Where the wool trade brought prosperity, elegant Georgian houses grace the village streets with their rounded bows and pillared doorways.

For this book I have chosen villages from throughout the county which, apart from their attractiveness, have a special appeal and should provide you with a memorable visit. All are set in wonderfully varied countryside. For example, in the New Forest you will discover the tiny settlement of Fritham, still remote and peaceful, surrounded by wide heaths and ancient yew woods. By contrast, field paths from Meonstoke in its lovely river valley lead you to the glorious open downland of Old Winchester Hill offering splendid views as far as the Solent.

And whatever your interests, I hope you will find your walk rewarding. History comes alive as you follow the tow path beside the Basingstoke canal from Greywell to the ruins of a castle built by King John, or cross the down near Martin along the ramparts of the great defensive earthwork of Bokerley Ditch raised by Celtic tribes in the 5th century. Tranquil Titchfield close to the Meon shore lies beside one of the county's finest Nature Reserves and the path from Buriton leads through the Queen Elizabeth Country Park, equally rich in wildlife. You can walk in the footsteps of Jane Austen in the countryside around her home at Chawton and climb the Zig-Zag path cut by Gilbert White up Selborne Hanger to share the splendid view he enjoyed on summer evenings. If you love gardens you can combine your walk beside the Test at Mottisfont with a visit to the National Trust's glorious collection of old-fashioned roses in the garden of Mottisfont Abbey. These are just some of the delights that await you in this fascinating county.

All the walks in this book are circular, ranging in length from 3 to 6½ miles and suitable for the family. They are accompanied by simple sketch maps designed to guide you to the starting point and give an overall picture of the route. For more detailed information arm yourself with the relevant Ordnance Survey Landranger map noted in the introduction to each walk. Or for a larger scale, 1: 25 000, use their Explorer maps which are replacing the Pathfinder series. Places where food and drink can be obtained are also given together with phone numbers so you can check opening times. You will find a note on nearby attractions – with phone numbers – at the end of each chapter. Car parking locations are indicated in the text, but if these are full or for some reason unusable, we are asked to respect the villagers' way of life and park carefully so as not to cause an obstruction.

Writing this book about my home county has been a great pleasure. I hope you will share that pleasure and enjoy many happy hours following these walks in Hampshire's beautiful countryside.

Anne-Marie Edwards
Ashurst
www.walksbooks.com

BURLEY

Length: 5 miles

Getting there: Burley is a large village in the south-west corner of the New Forest. Approach from the north via the A31 Ringwood-Cadnam road, turning for Burley at Picket Post or from the south via the A35

Christchurch-Lyndhurst road.

Parking: Drive into the village, to the Queen's Head and turn into the large free car park beside the pub car park. If this is full there are car parks up the

road opposite the pub, either side leading to the A35.

Maps: OS Landranger 195 Bournemouth & Purbeck; OS Outdoor Leisure 22 (GR 212 031)

Half-hidden in woods and approached in the past by lonely moorland paths, Burley was once so remote that it depended for its livelihood on its yearly crop of acorns and beech mast! But today this attractive village is one of the most popular in the Forest. Some of the houses are very old,

half-timbered behind a modern façade. The oldest is the Queen's Head pub which dates from the 17th century and was once a favourite haunt for smugglers.

Burley is sheltered to the west by a high ridge of moorland crowned by an Iron Age hill fort. The walk leads up Burley

Hill to the ramparts of the fort giving wonderful views. Then we follow a quiet road over wide heathland before taking tree-shaded meadow paths back to the village.

THE WALK

Before starting the walk look over the meadow on the right for a fine view of Burley Manor, now a hotel. It is likely a manor stood here in Saxon times as no further grants of land would have been made after William the Conqueror enclosed the Forest in 1079. A Tudor house on the site was replaced by a Georgian manor which was burnt down in 1850. After the fire Colonel Esdaile had the house rebuilt in Tudor style.

❶ With the manor over the fields on your right and the back of the Queen's Head on your left, leave the car park through a wooden gate to walk to the village street. Turn right and follow the pavement as far as Clough Lane. Cross the road and take the raised footpath signed Burley Street running parallel with the road. Follow this until it rejoins the road. Cross over and continue for about 50 yards to the gates of Burley Hill House on the left.

❷ Turn left, go through the right-hand gate and follow the fenced footpath which runs beside the drive then over bridges before winding gently up Burley Hill. Cross a stile and turn right along a track past Black Bush cottages. The track dips a little then rises to run across the centre of the Iron Age fort. At the top of the rise leave the track and turn left along the earth ramparts to enjoy the wonderful view west over the Avon valley to the distant outline of the Purbeck hills.

❸ Return to the track and turn left. Ignore the first track on the right but take the next one which leads downhill to meet the road in Burley Street. Turn right past the former shop and post office.

❹ Turn left down Forest Road signed 'Lyndhurst via ford'. This quiet lane bears right to cross Burley Moor with open heathland on the left overlooked by houses on the right. Walk along the soft turf beside the road for about ¾ mile.

❺ Just before the road turns sharp right, bear half-left over the grass to the fence at the corner of South Oakley Inclosure. Keep ahead with the fence on your left to cross a parking area and meet a minor road. Cross over and turn right along Mill Lane.

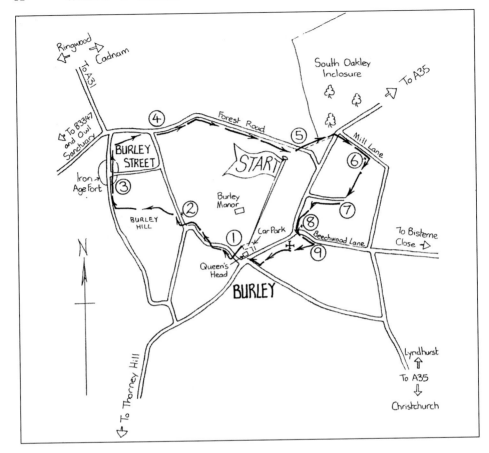

❻ After about ¼ mile look carefully for an iron gate and footpath sign on the right. Turn right through the gate to follow a grassy path through another gate, along the side of a paddock and over a double stile to continue through meadows full of wild flowers. Cross a bridge over a stream and continue over small concrete bridges to follow the path through a wood. The path bears right to a gravel track.

❼ Bear right along the track towards a row of houses. Turn left along the track in front of the houses (before you come to a road) and continue past a barrier with the houses on your right. Follow the edge of the Forest green, then bear a little right to meet a road.

❽ Turn left beside the road for about 200 yards, then turn left again along Beechwood Lane. Follow the lane to the point where Church Lane joins on the right.

❾ Turn right up Church Lane and when it divides continue along the right-hand track. Pass another track on the left to walk through a wood of massive oaks and

Horse-drawn waggonette rides along the Forest lanes start from the Queen's Head pub in Burley.

beeches to the church. Dedicated to St John the Baptist and consecrated by Charles Sumner, Bishop of Winchester, in 1839, this simple little church is particularly light and welcoming. The windows and memorial tablets tell their stories of Burley people. One inscription reads 'Emma Harding, 1873-1976, a faithful member of this congregation who continued to walk to church when past her hundredth year'. Opposite the church gate turn left up a track which passes the school on the right to meet a road. Turn right down the road to descend to the Queen's Head and your car park.

MINSTEAD

Length: 3 miles (to include a walk round Furzey Gardens)

Getting there: Minstead is a small village in the heart of the New Forest about 5 miles north of Lyndhurst. Turn for Minstead off the A337 Cadnam-Lyndhurst road. Follow the minor road through the Forest for a little over a mile then turn right for

the village centre when you see the village sign.

Parking: In the parking area on the right opposite the village green. If this is full, turn left following the sign for the church past the front of the

Trusty Servant pub, and park under the trees in front of the churchyard.

Maps: OS Landranger 195 Bournemouth & Purbeck; OS Outdoor Leisure 22 (GR 282110).

Minstead is an enchanting New Forest village composed of several small farming communities rambling around a network of thickly hedged lanes. Throughout the Forest houses tend to appear in unexpected places because in the past would-be residents could claim 'squatter's rights' if

they could build a home with a fireplace without being noticed by the authorities! So Minstead's special charm is its setting. The village's lush green meadows are surrounded by the still medieval landscape of the Forest, great oak and beech woods and wide expanses of heathland. This walk is a fascinating exploration of both worlds.

Starting from the village green, meadow paths and quiet lanes lead through undulating countryside to Furzey Gardens, beautiful gardens at their loveliest in spring (open from 10 am to 5 pm). Here you can discover how Forest workers lived in the past by visiting a carefully preserved 16th century cottage. The cottage has only two tiny bedrooms but at one time it housed 14 children! Paths through ancient woodland lead back to the village; passing one of the Forest's most interesting churches.

THE WALK

❶ With the village green on your left and the parking area on your right walk up the road past the side of the Trusty Servant pub. The unusual inn sign, copied from a picture in Winchester College, depicts 'the trusty servant'. He is a pig with a padlocked snout to illustrate discretion and stag's feet to indicate speed in running errands! Just past the pub turn right down a lane which threads its way between meadows shaded by massive Forest trees. After about 200 yards turn left following a footpath sign along an attractive path which curves right through a small wooden gate. The path ahead is a long green tunnel burrowing beneath arching branches. Follow it through another wooden gate to meet a lane. Turn left and follow the lane round to the right to a T-junction.

❷ Turn left down Seamans Lane passing some of the isolated houses of London Minstead – a most inappropriate name as you will discover! The lane runs for about ¼ mile to meet a road at Seamans Corner.

❸ Turn left and continue for about 100 yards past Minstead Village Hall, then turn right down a lane signed for Furzey Gardens. The lane climbs to a track on the left leading to the entrance to the gardens.

❹ Take the left turn and enjoy a ramble round this lovely hillside garden. Tiny paths wind among pools and pergolas brilliant with massed rhododendrons, azaleas and a host of other plants which flourish on the acid soil. The 16th century cottage is close to the entrance and there is also a large gallery displaying Forest arts and crafts. Turn left from the garden entrance to continue the walk and follow the signed path through the woods for a short distance to another footpath sign. Here the path divides. Take the right-hand path which runs downhill to pass between wooden posts and over a footbridge. Pass more wooden posts and continue over a

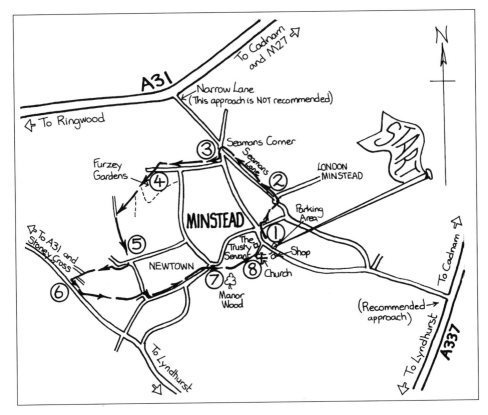

sequence of causeways to cross a stile. Continue uphill to a crosspath. Turn left over a stile. A narrow fenced path dips and rises beside fields before leading you over another stile, past a house on the left to a lane.

❺ Cross the stile and turn right following the bridleway sign. When the track divides continue along the left-hand track which climbs gently to another division. Again take the left-hand track and continue past a lane on the left to a minor road.

❻ Turn left beside the road for just a few yards, then bear left past a barrier, follow-

ing a bridleway sign, over the grass to enter woods. Now a beautiful path leads downhill, curving a little left past lanes to left and right to meet the road in Newtown. You will see a telephone box on the right. Bear left beside the road and follow it as it curves left and descends to a ford. Cross the footbridge beside the ford.

❼ Leave the road and bear half-right for a few yards to a gate and footpath sign on the left leading into Manor Wood. Walk up through the wood, then follow the field

path which climbs past Minstead's fascinating church. From the outside,

This 400 year old cottage close to the entrance to Furzey Gardens has been carefully preserved to show how Forest workers lived in the past.

brick-built extensions give it a cottage-like appearance but inside you will find much of interest including an old gallery and a rare three-decker pulpit. At the southern end of the churchyard a stone cross marks the grave of Sir Arthur Conan Doyle, the creator of Sherlock Holmes. The author lived at Bignell Wood close by and wrote about Minstead in one of his novels, *The White Company*.

❽ Follow the lane from the church gate past the war memorial on the village green and so back to your car.

FRITHAM

Length: 5 miles

Getting there: The best approach is via the B3078 Brook-Fordingbridge road. From the Cadnam roundabout take the B3079 signed for Fritham. Just past the Bell Inn in Brook take the left-hand road at the fork, B3078, signed Fording-bridge. After about 1½ miles turn left and shortly after turn right for Fritham.

Parking: Drive down the lane past the Royal Oak pub and turn left into the parking area.

Maps: OS Landranger 195 Bournemouth & Purbeck, OS Outdoor Leisure 22 (GR 231141)

It is hard to imagine a more peaceful place than Fritham. This small hamlet tucked away behind wide green lawns in the remote north-west corner of the New Forest seems little changed since it appeared as 'Thorougham' in the Domesday Book. But during the 19th century this quiet village was at the centre of a thriving industry with workers arriving from as far away as Downton and Fordingbridge. Schultze gunpowder works, making powder for sporting guns, was established in the valley close by at Eyeworth. Narrow Forest tracks were embanked and strengthened to take the weight of huge carts drawn by teams of heavy horses and the stream through the valley was dammed to make a pond for cooling purposes. The works closed in 1910 and today Fritham, with its surrounding oak and beech woods overlooking Eyeworth pond, is one of the loveliest places in the Forest.

All aspects of the beautiful New Forest can be enjoyed on this walk. The route

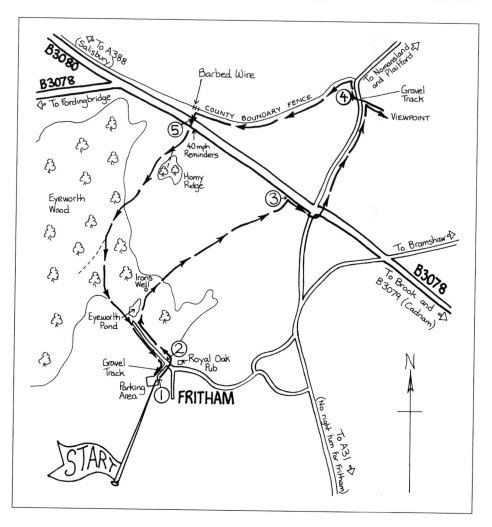

Eyeworth Pond.

follows the bank of the pond and continues along a wide green valley to cross the heath to a magnificent viewpoint. Grassy paths through scattered woodland lead high on the heath again before descending through the ancient trees of Eyeworth Wood and returning to the village.

THE WALK

❶ From the parking area return to the metalled lane, past a gravelled track on the left. Just before the lane you will see an iron postbox on the left. It was placed here before 1900 to save the postman the walk down to the Schultze factory. The postman delivered and collected the mail – a penny for a letter and a halfpenny for newspapers – every day except Sunday.

❷ Turn left and follow the metalled lane

downhill to enjoy a beautiful view of Eyeworth Pond. Turn right to walk beside the pond with the pond on your left. You might like to linger here and watch families of ducks paddle about happily among carpets of waterlilies and stands of yellow irises. Keep straight ahead past the barrier. After about 200 yards you will see wooden palings surrounding the reddish brown waters of Irons Well on the left. In the past this chalybeate spring was considered beneficial for sore eyes. Follow the embanked path through woods and along the valley. The path rises gently to cross heathland and reach a road, the B3078.

❸ Turn right to walk over the heath beside the road for about 150 yards to a crossroads. Turn left to follow the route of the minor road heading north. Make your way over the heath with the minor road close on your left – it is very pleasant walking – for about ¾ mile to the corner of a gravel track on the right. Make a short detour here to enjoy a viewpoint by turning right to cross the heath to the right of the road. Continue for about 300 yards to the point where a valley opens out on the left giving a splendid view over massed woodlands to the soft blue haze of the downs. Retrace your steps to the corner of the gravel track and continue down the minor road to where the road makes a sharp right-hand bend.

❹ Turn left off the corner up a gravel track past a house on the right. The fence on the right marks the county boundary with Wiltshire and is our guide for the next part of the walk. Pass a barrier and follow the path as it dips and rises across a valley and through woods. The path is indistinct at times but keep the boundary fence within 30 yards of you on the right. Continue for about a mile. The B3078 will now be running almost parallel with your path about 50 yards away over the heath on your left. Look carefully for a narrow path leading left to the road just beyond two shield-shaped 40 mph reminder signs, and right to the boundary fence blocked by strands of barbed wire.

❺ Take this narrow path on the left to the road close to the signs. Cross the road and follow the grassy path leading past a barrier and over the heath towards the wood on Homy Ridge. The path bears right to leave the wood on the left. When the path divides take the right-hand path to skirt the wood. Continue along the

---

PLACES of INTEREST

Close to Brook, signed from the village and from the A31, stands the **Rufus Stone** said to mark the spot where the oak tree stood, in 1100, from which an arrow glanced to strike King William II (William Rufus). He died instantly.

Paulton's Park at Ower, near Cadnam, is a large family leisure park with a variety of play areas and amusements including a miniature railway. Restaurant and tearooms. Open mid March to October 10 am to 6.30 pm. Earlier closing in spring and autumn. Telephone: 023 8081 4455.

---

path as it enters Eyeworth Wood and keep to the main track as it curves left through the trees. When the path divides, take the left-hand path which eventually leads out of the wood past a barrier and some houses on the right. The last house with bay windows was formerly the home of the manager of the Schultze works. Cross the bridge over the stream and continue along the lane with the pond on your left. Follow the lane uphill and turn right into the parking area at Fritham.

MARTIN

Length: 4½ miles

Getting there: Martin is in north-west Hampshire south of Salisbury. Approaching from the west turn for Martin off the A354. The best approach from the east is via the A338 through Fordingbridge. From Fording-bridge follow the B3078 to Damerham, then follow the

signs for Martin, about 4 miles north-west.

Parking: Drive into the village and turn up a narrow metalled lane opposite the village hall. (The hall looks like a chapel with pointed windows.) The lane leads to the church where

there is a large parking area on the right before the gate into the churchyard. There is a sign for the church on the right pointing up the lane but it may be obscured.

Map: OS Landranger 184 Salisbury (GR 070195).

Martin is one of Hampshire's loveliest villages. It lies in a shallow valley in the chalk downs close to the border with Dorset and Wiltshire. A long curving road runs through the village edged by grassy banks where single rows of houses and cot-

tages face each other over beautifully-tended gardens. All the houses are different and all are fascinating. Most are dark thatched and many are timber-framed. And this is a village of flowers. Hollyhocks seem determined to reach into

FOOD and DRINK

There is nowhere to purchase a meal or snack in Martin so I would suggest a visit to The Compasses pub in nearby Damerham. Telephone: 01725 518231.

based on that of a real shepherd, William Lawes, whose gravestone stands prominently in front of the church tower.

If you love wildlife, flowers and birdsong then do not miss this walk! Just south of Martin is a 900 acre nature reserve, one of the most extensive areas of unploughed chalk downland in the country. The walk follows a pleasant lane to the reserve, then climbs the down to Bokerley Ditch. This great earthwork with ramparts still 40 feet high in places, probably dates from early in the 5th century and was built by Roman-

upstairs windows and great masses of roses spill over walls. The naturalist W. H. Hudson wrote about Martin, which he called Winterbourne Bishop, in his book *A Shepherd's Life* published in 1910. His account of the life of Isaac Bawcombe is

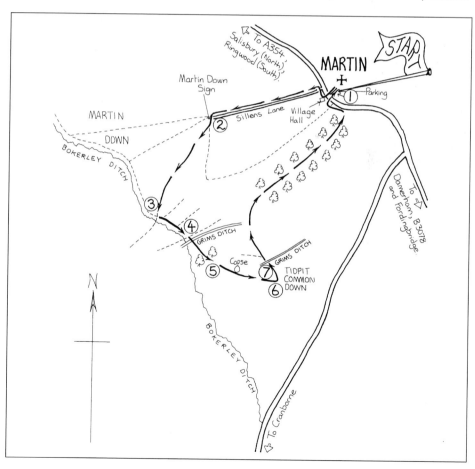

ised Celts in an attempt to prevent the westward advance of invading Saxon armies. We follow the Ditch along the crest of the down over another, even older earthwork, Grim's Ditch, before taking more grassy paths over Tidpit Down and returning to Martin along an attractive tree-shaded way.

THE WALK

❶ With your back to the church, walk down the lane to the road and turn right, leaving the village hall on your left. Turn left just before the green along Sillens Lane. Follow the lane for about a mile to Martin Down Nature Reserve.

❷ When the tarmac ends, leave the car park on your right and follow the track bearing left for just a few yards. At this point the track divides. Take the right-hand track which winds gently up the down through grassland bright with wild flowers. In spring the down is golden with cowslips and in summer you will see all the flowers of the chalk including burnt-tip orchids and yellow horseshoe vetch which looks like tiny sweet peas. Butterflies fluttering in the longer grass include the dark green fritillary and marbled white. As you gain height and cross the short turf you should see the silver spotted skipper and Adonis blue. Flocks of dark Hebridean sheep graze on the hillside. Continue to the top of the down to face Bokerley Ditch.

❸ A track cuts across the earthwork in front of you. Do not take this (into Dorset!) but turn left to walk along the

Bokerley Ditch.

crest of the down with the ditch and the high rampart behind it on your right. Keep ahead past two paths on the left leading downhill. On your left is a wide view over a patchwork of undulating fields and copses with Martin church spire rising from among the trees. The path curves right uphill. Ignore all other paths and continue ahead keeping Bokerley Ditch close on your right.

❹ At the top of the rise you come to a crosspath. Go straight over to cross a shallow trench running at right angles to Bokerley Ditch. This is Grim's Ditch, possibly part of a system of land enclosure dating back to 1,000 BC. The path now weaves through scrub and oak woods which provide shelter and food for a wide variety of birds including warblers and nightingales. Continue for about ¼ mile to a small wooden gate.

❺ There is no clear path at this point but go through the gate and follow the direction indicated by the blue arrow bridleway sign, to bear half-left diagonally up the field ahead to the right-hand corner of a small copse. Continue down the field still bearing half-left aiming for a wire fence on

your left. Follow the line of the fence into the dip at the foot of the field to gates on your left.

❻ Turn left through the gate.

❼ Follow a rather indistinct path along a shallow valley, Tidpit Common Down. The path climbs to follow the hillside to a gate leading to Martin Down. Go through to cross Grim's Ditch once more and take the right-hand path when the way divides. Descend the hillside keeping to the same path as it curves a little right and becomes a track leading back to Martin. Turn left when you come to the road to walk through the village, then right to return to your car.

BREAMORE

Length: 4 miles

Getting there: Breamore lies in the Avon valley beside the A338 Salisbury – Ringwood road, 3 miles north of Fordingbridge. Drive into the village and turn west along a lane signed for Breamore House and church.

After about ⅓ mile when the lane bears left keep straight on along a narrower lane signed for the church, to a T-junction. Turn left for a few yards, then turn right following the car park sign.

Parking: In the large free car park indicated at the entrance to the Tea Barn and Museum.

Map: OS Landranger 184 Salisbury (GR 152188).

Breamore presents an idyllic picture. Timber-framed thatched cottages cluster around a large common, overlooked by an Elizabethan manor house surrounded by beautiful parkland. This forms the perfect setting for a wonderful church, built by the Saxons in the 10th century. The manor,

Breamore House, is built of warm red brick, and was completed in 1583 by William Dodington, Auditor of the Tower Mint. Later the house and estate were sold to King George II's physician, Sir Edward Hulse, and it is still the Hulse family home. Inside you will find a fine collection of furniture and the wood-panelled Great Hall is hung with paintings by Dutch artists of the 17th and 18th centuries.

Do not miss a visit to the church. Much of the Saxon fabric survives, showing typical 'long and short' stone work and deep-splayed round-topped windows. Above the south door is a Saxon sculpture and the arch leading into the south transept bears an inscription in Anglo-Saxon which translates as 'Here is made plain the covenant to thee'.

This is an easy walk which all the family will enjoy. There is an opportunity to visit the manor and the church before woodland paths lead to the open downs. A grassy path leads to Breamore's mysterious Miz Maze formed by eleven concentric rings of turf, possibly medieval in origin. Field paths descend the downs and lanes lead through the village to return to the car park.

THE WALK

❶ From the car park walk past the entrance sign into a courtyard. The Countryside Museum is on your right. You can buy a combined ticket here to visit the Museum and Breamore House. Pass the Tea Barn on your right and turn right along a gravel track. After about 150 yards you come to the columns surmounted by stone lions at the approach to Breamore Park. The walk turns left here, following the bridleway sign up the drive, but to see the church keep straight on to the gate into the churchyard on the left. To resume the walk, retrace your steps to the entrance to the Park. Follow the drive through the park past Breamore House on your right. Keep straight ahead into Breamore Wood when the way becomes a gravel track.

❷ Follow the track as it climbs gently between fine oak, beech, sweet chestnut and yew trees. One mighty pollarded chestnut has no fewer than five huge trunks! Continue for about ¾ mile, to leave the woods at the top of the hill. Look left to enjoy beautiful views over undulating fields and copses to the Dorset downs.

❸ Shortly you meet a crossing track. Turn left to descend to the foot of a hillside. Take the grassy track straight up the

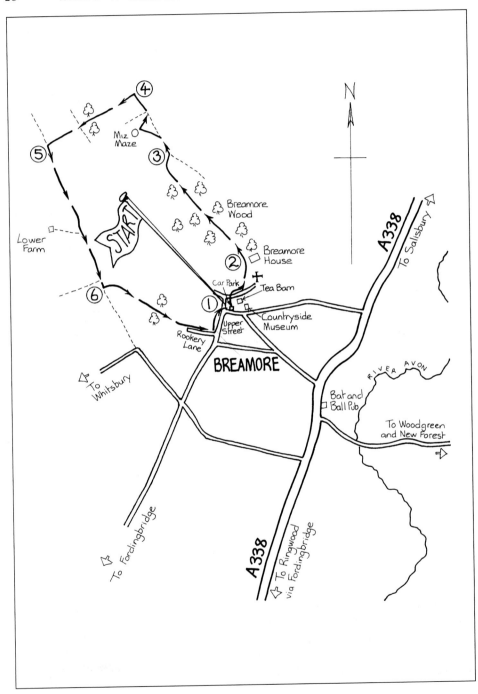

The wonderful Saxon church at Breamore.

hill signed with the Countryside Commission's white arrow on a green background, to a white notice indicating the way to the Miz Maze. Turn left through the yew trees to see the maze. Retrace your steps to the notice and turn left to resume your former heading. Follow the path as it descends the hillside and curves right to a T-junction. Turn left and continue past a permissive footpath sign and a stile on the left. About 100 yards further on you will see another stile on the left.

❹ Turn left over this stile and follow the wide grassy path down the side of a field to walk through a wood. Pass a barn on the right and keep straight ahead over a crosstrack. The path continues downhill to a stile.

❺ Cross the stile and turn left along another grassy track. Pass an iron gate to meet a gravel track and follow this straight ahead. Continue past the drive to Lower Farm. After about ¼ mile you pass a bridleway sign on the right. Keep ahead for about 30 yards to a footpath sign on the left.

The mysterious Miz Maze on Breamore Down.

❻ Turn left to follow a narrow path up a gully with a field on your left and a hedge on your right. Cross the stile at the top of the field and follow a sunken path through woods. Go straight over a crosspath to continue along Rookery Lane. Turn left at the end of Rookery Lane into Upper Street to see some of Breamore's most attractive houses. They include a fine Jacobean building known as the Rookery, named like the street after the Rooke family who rose from tenant farmers to gentry. Follow Upper Street as it curves right and turn left to return to the car park.

MOTTISFONT

Length: 5½ miles

Getting there: Mottisfont is a small village in the valley of the River Test 4 miles north of Romsey. Turn for Mottisfont off the A3057 and drive for about a mile into the village.

Parking: You can leave your car in the large National Trust car park which is clearly signed on the right as you approach the village. However, the car park is closed at 6 pm, or dusk whichever is the earlier. There is a small parking area near the church. Continue past the entrance to the National Trust car park and take the first lane on the left, Church Lane. The parking area is almost immediately on your left.

Map: OS Landranger 185 Winchester & Basingstoke (GR 325268).

This charming village of mellow brick and thatch situated among meadows and woods on the west bank of the River Test, dates back to Saxon times. The village name is derived from the Saxon word for a meeting place, a moot, which was beside a spring, or font. The spring still rises to form a deep pool in the grounds of Mottisfont Abbey. The mansion, now the property of the National Trust, incorporates part of an early 13th century Augustinian priory. The beautiful grounds

FOOD and DRINK

Unfortunately the Mottisfont Tea Room is now closed but, for refreshments half-way round the walk, I recommend the Mill Arms at Dunbridge which offers a warm welcome to walkers. Telephone: 01794 340401.

are crossed by a branch of the river Test which flows serenely through lawns shaded by ancient trees. But pride of place must go to the splendid collection of old-fashioned roses planted by the National Trust in the former walled kitchen garden.

Just south of Mottisfont the River Dun flows into the Test. This very pleasant walk follows part of the Test Way footpath and then heads west through the meadows of the Dun valley. Woodland paths climb to give wide views over rolling downland before we cross the fields to return to Mottisfont.

THE WALK

❶ If you have parked in the National Trust car park, turn right from the entrance, walk up the village street and turn left into Church Lane. Follow the lane past the church on your left. From the parking area near the church, just continue along the lane, church on your left. The church of St Andrew has lovely 15th century stained glass. Pass some thatched cottages and keep straight on down a grassy track. Cross a stile and continue over a field to an iron gate.

❷ Go through the gate and cross the bridge over the River Dun. This clear chalk

The River Dun flows swiftly through the meadows near Mottisfont.

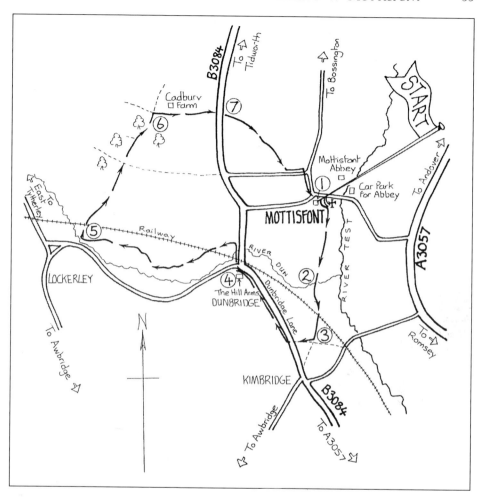

stream is particularly beautiful here, flowing swiftly through the meadows between tree-shaded banks. After another gate the path leads uphill through woods to meet a track. Turn right over the railway bridge and walk through woods to a crosstrack.

❸ Turn right and continue through a gate, past some houses in Kimbridge to meet Dunbridge Lane. Turn right and follow the lane for just over ½ mile into Dunbridge. (After the first 100 yards there is a grass verge and later a footpath.)

❹ Opposite the Mill Arms, follow the B3084 turning right signed for Mottisfont. Cross the railway and the bridge over the Dun and after about 30 yards turn left down a wide track. Continue through a gate and keep ahead over a stile to cross the railway and the stile on the other side. Follow the track past an electricity substation on the right. On the left meadows lead to the river framed by wooded hills. Go through a gate and cross the field where another gate leads you to a charming thatched cottage. Leave the cottage on your right and follow a narrow path over rough meadow land between high hedges to a more open area. The path now bears a little right, then curves left to cross a plank bridge between stiles to another meadow. Keep straight ahead beside the meadow, with a row of trees on your right, to cross two footbridges over a marshy area. The path now bears slightly left towards the river. Go through a small gate to a track.

❺ Do not cross the river but turn right and follow the track to go under the railway. When the track ceases keep straight on, following a narrow path beside fields with hedges on your right. The path swings left towards woodland. At the entrance to the wood cross the stile by the National Trust sign and keep straight ahead through the trees. At the end of the wood go straight over a crosspath and the field ahead to cross a plank bridge and enter oak woods. Turn right at the crossing path to follow an enchanting path which

climbs gently through the trees for about ¼ mile to a crosstrack.

❻ Turn right (no sign but it is a right-of-way) to leave the woods and follow the track past Cadbury Farm to meet the B3084.

❼ Cross the road, go past a gate and follow the path bearing half-right diagonally across a field towards a line of trees and another footpath sign. Continue over the next field. The roofs of Mottisfont village appear ahead. Bear right for a few yards to a lane then turn left to meet a road. Turn right to walk back to the Tea Room and Post Office and your car.

PLACES of INTEREST

Mottisfont Abbey and Gardens are open from April to October, Saturday to Wednesday 12 am to 6 pm; in June also Thursday to 8.30 pm. Telephone: 01794 341220.
  Hillier Gardens and Arboretum, comprising one of the finest collections of trees and shrubs in England, are nearby at Ampfield. Open all year Monday to Friday 10 am to 5 pm, also weekends from March to the second Sunday in November. Telephone: 01794 368787.

WHERWELL
Length: 6½ miles

Getting There: Wherwell is a small village in the Test valley about 4 miles south of Andover. Turn for the village from the A3057 Andover-Romsey road, or if approaching from the east turn off the A303 along the

B3048. From Winchester head north along the B3420.

Parking: Drive into the village and turn by the war memorial (a small cenotaph) down Church Street. Turn left into the car

park just before the entrance into the churchyard.

Map: OS Landranger 185 Winchester & Basingstoke (GR 391408).

Wherwell is an enchanting village of deep-thatched houses and cottages, many half-timbered with dazzlingly white walls. The river Test flows swiftly past colourful gardens, swirling around islands hung with willows. It is difficult to imagine a more peaceful place but this quiet village has a

turbulent history. In AD 986 an abbey was founded here not by some saintly cleric but by a wicked stepmother! Queen Elfrida, widow of King Edgar, in an attempt to ease her conscience after murdering her stepson at Corfe Castle, chose the village for her abbey possibly because

---

FOOD and DRINK

The White Lion serves excellent meals in a
friendly atmosphere. Telephone: 01264 860317.

---

it was close to her first home in Harewood
Forest. At the Dissolution the buildings
were destroyed and a large house built on
the site. Held by Royalists during the Civil
War, the house was besieged by Oliver
Cromwell. Today you will find it replaced
by an early 19th century house, the Priory.
Little of the Abbey remains but if you look
carefully you will spot pieces of carved
stonework in some house walls!

Although this ramble is quite long it is
very easy walking with no steep gradients.
Footpaths lead from Wherwell over the
downs to give wide views over the valley
of the river Anton. We follow the river,
then take a track through a lovely area of
Harewood Forest before returning to the
village along a tree-shaded footpath.

THE WALK
❶ Turn right from the car park up
Church Street, and at the top turn left.
Keep ahead through the village past a road
on the right, following the sign for Stock-
bridge. Continue for about ¼ mile to a
footpath sign on the left. Turn left to enjoy
a beautiful view of the river crossed by
wooden footbridges. Retrace your steps to
the road and turn left to resume your
former heading for about 60 yards.

❷ Turn right following the footpath sign
and climb the steps. The path bears left
(ignore a stile on the right) beside a field
with a hedge on the left. Continue for 100

yards then descend the bank on the left to
a wide green track. Bear right to follow the
track uphill between fields. The track
bears round to the right, then left. At the
top of the hill turn right (the 'Private'
notice applies to the path ahead) and
follow the hedged path downhill. The
path bears briefly left then right. Follow
the path as it skirts a field along the top of
a bank with a hedge on the right. Go
through a small wooden gate and continue
along the side of open downland for about
100 yards.

❸ Bearing a little right walk diagonally
down the hillside to go through another
small wooden gate to a road, the A3057.

❹ Cross the road and follow the track
ahead, a hedge on the left. Go through an
iron gate and keep straight on through a
belt of woodland. Keep the hedge on the
left as you continue beside another field.
Now the path becomes an earth track as it
bears slightly right and runs through trees,
with the river Anton at this point hidden
by bushes on the left. Follow the track for
about a mile, across an open area then
through an iron gate to continue through
woods with glimpses of the river. Go
through another iron gate to the road in
Goodworth Clatford.

❺ Turn right to walk up the road past the
church on the left to the A3057. Cross
straight over and take the bridleway ahead
over a crossing track. The path climbs
between high hedges with a golf course on
the right. Ignore all the gravel turnings
into the golf course and continue to a
grassy crossing track.

The River Test is at its loveliest as it flows beneath the willows at Wherwell.

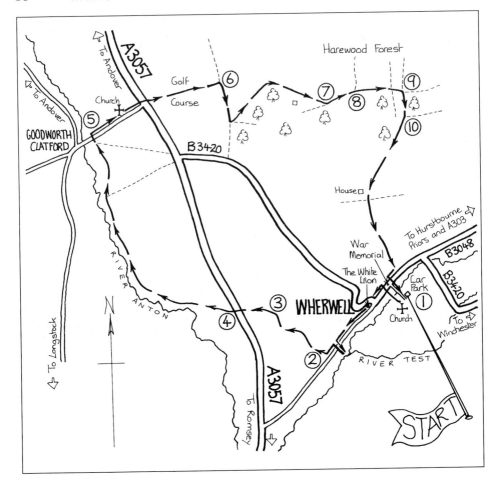

❻ Turn right along the track towards the woods and as you reach the trees look for a footpath sign on the left. Turn left and bear left when the path divides. Keep ahead with the woods on your right and a fringe of hazels on your left. The path leaves the trees in front of a keeper's cottage on the right. Bear a little left then resume your former heading to walk beside a field, the hedge on your right, to a concrete track.

❼ Keep ahead along the concrete track for about ¼ mile. Now you need to navigate carefully!

❽ Leave the concrete track just before it bends left to enter woods and take the path to the right of it. (If you follow the concrete track round the corner there is a large Private sign so you know to turn back!) Now the path leads along a shallow valley to enter Harewood Forest and becomes a wide green way. Go straight

Fungus decorates a beech tree in Harewood Forest.

over a crosspath by a wooden footpath marker post and continue for about 50 yards to another post at a crosspath.

❾ Turn right to follow an earth path which climbs through the trees to emerge into the open at a crossing path.

❿ Bear right and follow the path as it swings left with woods on the right. Keep straight on over a crosspath and keep to the path as it continues past a house on the right. Cross a track and keep ahead over a rise to descend between hedges and

---

PLACES of INTEREST

North of Wherwell, approached by a beech avenue from the A303 Andover Road, is **Deadman's Plack**. This commemorates the murder of Elfrida's first husband, Ethelwulf. Sent by King Edgar to assess Elfrida as a possible wife, Ethelwulf succumbed to her charm and married her himself. Discovering what had happened, Edgar killed Ethelwulf and made Elfrida his Queen.

---

go under the disused railway bridge to the road in Wherwell. Turn right for a few yards to the war memorial, then turn left down Church Street to return to your car.

AMPORT

Length: 5 miles

Getting there: Amport is a small village about 4 miles west of Andover. Turn off the A303 Andover Bypass following the sign for Monxton and drive through Monxton to Amport which is a little further down the lane. Approaching from the A343, follow the sign for Abbotts Ann, bear left in the village for Monxton and continue to Amport.

Parking: Drive into the village past the Amport Inn and the Sarson Lane turning to pass the large village green on your right. A row of cottages faces the green on your left. At the far side of the green turn right by the telephone box and park on the hard standing beside the gravel track facing the green.

Maps: OS Landrangers: 184 Salisbury; and Winchester & Basingstoke 185 (GR 303443).

Amport, with its thatched cottages and tree-fringed green set in the wide valley of the Pillhill Brook, is one of my favourite villages. There is a special charm about this quiet place where people have lived and worked for 5,000 years. The Saxons built a village here and some of the straight tracks across the fields were once Roman roads. Until the end of the 19th century the tracks carried huge flocks of sheep to the important fair at Weyhill, 2 miles north of the village. Here Thomas

Hardy witnessed the sale of a wife and child for £5, an event which he wove into his novel *The Mayor of Casterbridge*.

Hardy would still recognise the gently undulating countryside dotted with ancient woods. The route follows the Pillhill Brook then heads west along a remarkably straight track to Quarley, another old world village. A beautiful grassy path runs beside woods to a quiet lane which leads past a Gothic mansion, Amport House, to return to the village green.

THE WALK

❶ With your back to the houses, follow the gravel track with the village green on your right. Pass a cottage on your right. Continue along a path with the Pillhill Brook running through meadows on the right and a hedge on the left to cross a stile. You pass the remains of former watercress beds, then the path bears left uphill. Cross the stile at the top to a field.

❷ Turn left up the edge of the field, keeping a hedge on your left for about 50 yards. Then bear right with a wood on your left for a few yards to the corner of the wood. Bear left, still keeping the wood close on your left. Continue round the edge of the field beside the wood to meet a wide grassy crosspath. (There is a yellow arrow footpath sign on a post on the right.)

❸ Turn right and follow the wide path for about ¼ mile over Hay Down. In the WI publication *It happened in Hampshire* I read that houses were built here for people whom the Churchwardens considered 'might contaminate the more virtuous inhabitants of the village'! Continue to a track.

❹ Turn left to walk between some farm buildings. Keep straight on with a fence on the left. Pass a house on the left and continue along the edge of a field to cross a stile. Turn right for just a few yards and look for a footpath sign on the left.

❺ Turn left as the sign directs and follow the long straight path ahead, the hedge on the right, between fields for about ¾ mile. I believe this must be Roman in origin. On the horizon you will see Quarley hill fort. Originally an Iron Age camp, it was occupied by the Romans and is the only hill fort in Hampshire to have four entrances at opposite points in the Roman fashion. Go through a gate to a lane.

❻ Bear a little left to follow the lane for about ¼ mile until it curves left. Leave the lane and turn right past an iron gate to follow a wide green way past another iron gate to a road.

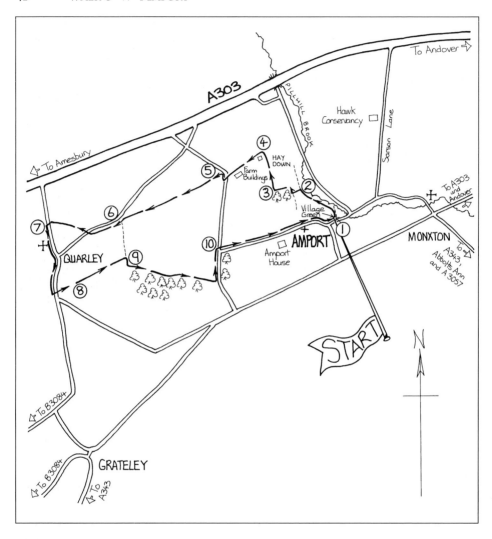

❼ Turn left to walk down this quiet road through the pretty village of Quarley. On the right, on a small hill, stands the tiny church of St Michael. The nave is 11th century and the chancel is lit by an early Venetian window. The heavy bells are hung in a shelter outside the north wall. Keep to the road as it curves right past the village hall then left past the war memorial. Pass the Old School House on the right and after about 50 yards just past Barn Close turn left before Corner Cottage to walk beside a row of half-timbered cottages down a lane which is my idea of a perfect medieval village street!

❽ Continue along a narrow path which leads through trees then follows the edge

The bells of Quarley church are in the churchyard protected by a low slate roof.

❽ Continue along a narrow path which leads through trees then follows the edge of a field with trees on the left. At the far end of the field turn right and keep ahead for about 50 yards to a stile on the left.

❾ Turn left over the stile and follow the path running beside woods on the right for about ¾ mile to pass an iron gate to a lane. Turn left along the lane with a wood on your right for about ¼ mile.

❿ When the wood ceases turn right past an iron gate down a green way. The wood is on your right. Keep ahead as the grass gives way to gravel and having passed another iron gate becomes metalled. On the right you pass Amport House. During the Second World War it was Headquarters, Royal Air Force Maintenance Command and now it is the home of the Royal Air Force Chaplains School. The road leads to a junction. Turn left to pass the school and return to the village green.

HURSTBOURNE TARRANT

Length: 4½ miles

Getting there: Hurstbourne Tarrant lies in the Bourne valley about 8 miles north of Andover. The A343 Andover-Newbury road runs through the village. A prettier approach, from the south, is to follow the A3057 from Romsey, turn right for Wherwell along the B3048 then keep to this road as it runs through to Hurstbourne Tarrant with lovely views of the Bourne valley along the way.

Parking: If approaching via the A343 turn right just past the George and Dragon Inn and park opposite the church. The B3048 runs past the church. Park on the left.

Map: OS Landranger 185 Winchester & Basingstoke (GR 385530).

Hurstbourne Tarrant is set in the hills of north-west Hampshire, a beautiful area often called 'the Hampshire Highlands'. William Cobbett, the author of *Rural Rides*, visiting his friend Joseph Blount at Rookery Farm, wrote that 'the village is a sight worth going many miles to see'. I think you will agree with him! The ancient church overlooks a cluster of brick and flint cottages, many half-timbered and thatched, and elegant 18th century houses set in smooth green lawns. Above the meadowland framing the village rise steep wooded hillsides. Jane Austen enjoyed

FOOD and DRINK

The George and Dragon Inn is a delightful old-world hostelry, with a really welcoming atmosphere and serving excellent family meals. Telephone: 01264 736277.

walking here with her friends Martha and Mary Lloyd who lived nearby at Ibthorpe House.

We walk in her footsteps from the church over the meadows to Ibthorpe. Then we take a path south of the village which leads gradually uphill between hedges wreathed in ivy and wild clematis. Wonderful views unfold as we near the

top. We follow a footpath through the ancient woodland of Doles Copse before descending Hurstbourne Hill to return to the church.

THE WALK

❶ Walk through the church gate into the churchyard. Keep ahead with the church tower on your right and a wall on your left for about 30 yards to a small iron gate on your left. Go through the gate and continue along the edge of a field to cross a stile. Walk ahead over the next field, passing a magnificent thatched barn, to a small iron gate. Through the gate a narrow path tunnels between trees to a gravel track. Follow this to the road, the A343.

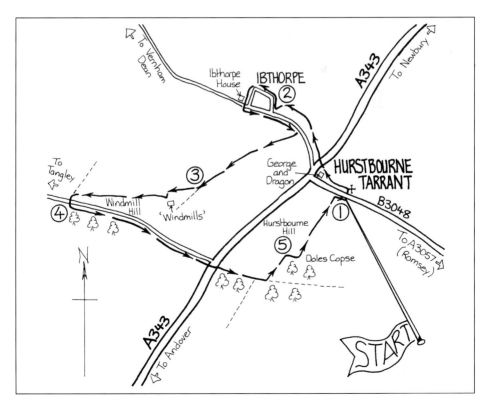

The Bourne valley from Hurstbourne Hill.

Cross, and take the footpath ahead. Bear a little right through an iron gate and follow the path straight on along the Bourne valley over the fields and through gates. A final gate leads to a farm track. Turn left then follow the track as it curves right to the lane in Ibthorpe.

❷ Turn right to walk round this horseshoe cluster of delightful thatched houses. Keep to the lane as it bears left to meet the main road, the B3048. On the corner, on the right, you will see Ibthorpe House. It is built of rose-coloured brick in the ordered classical style with neat rows of sash windows and a scroll-supported canopy over the front door. Turn left to walk beside the road towards Hurstbourne Tarrant. Pass the chapel and about 50 yards further on turn right opposite Toll Gate Cottage.

Walk up a track running past the side of Boundary Cottage. After a few yards the track becomes a green path. Follow this as it winds uphill for about ¾ mile and cross a stile. Now you are faced by two stiles.

❸ Turn right to cross the right-hand stile and follow the hedged path to another stile. Cross this into a field and keep ahead with trees on your left to go over another stile into a lane. Bear left for just a few yards to a stile and footpath sign on the right. Cross the stile and walk over the field, leaving a water tower (the adjacent buildings are now residential) on the right. Keep ahead through a narrow belt of woodland, go over a stile and continue across the next field. The path leads through more trees to take you over a final stile to meet a gravel track. Bear left to a lane.

❹ Turn left to follow this pleasant lane bordered by woods along the top of Windmill Hill. Opposite a house named 'Windmills' the trees break to reveal views to the south-west. From here, Jane Austen would have been able to see the countryside around her home at Steventon, not far from Basingstoke. The lane runs for about a mile to meet the A343. Cross straight over and take the footpath ahead through a gate. The path follows the edge of a wood on the right, then enters the trees of Doles Copse. Pass a green track on the right and continue through the wood for about 100 yards. Look carefully for a small post some yards into the bracken on the left, marked with three yellow arrow footpath signs. Turn left to walk to the post (the path could be faint). Follow the sign straight ahead. The path becomes clearer under the trees. This attractive woodland was coppiced in the past to provide the raw material for hurdle and

basket making. Follow the path as it descends to the corner of a fence. A path joins from the right. Ignore this and continue downhill with the fence on your left. The descent is rather steep but shortly you come to a field and now the going is easy.

❺ Turn right beside the wood on the right and follow the edge of the field round to the left down to a stile. Cross and walk over the recreation field to go over two stiles to a lane between the houses in Hurstbourne Tarrant. Cross a small bridge to the road and turn right for the church and your car.

HANNINGTON

Length: 5 miles

Getting there: Hannington is a small village in a fold of the North Hampshire Downs between Newbury and Basingstoke. Turn for Hannington off the A339 2 miles east of

Kingsclere. Follow the lane for 2½ miles, then bear left into the village to the village green, which is on your right.

Parking: Park by the village

green near the church.

Map: OS Landranger 174 Newbury & Wantage (GR 539555).

Hannington is a beautiful village of brick, flint and thatched houses half-hidden among tall trees and hedges. The magnificent green is overlooked by a Norman church and surrounded by farm buildings and cottages. It makes the perfect place for a picnic or just to relax after your walk. In the centre a pointed roof

covers a well head, installed in 1897 to commemorate Queen Victoria's Diamond Jubilee. A visit to the church is a 'must'. Some of the sturdy Norman pillars, built of solid chalk, are inscribed with Crusaders' crosses and there are two fine memorial windows engraved by Lawrence Whistler.

Just north of the village the high

downland falls away in a steep escarpment to give breathtaking views over the Thames valley. This walk climbs the down to enjoy the view, crossing the route of the Portway, the Roman road that formed part of the link between London and Salisbury (Old Sarum). We follow the edge of the escarpment for nearly 2 miles, passing the site of an ancient settlement, before taking field paths to return to Hannington.

THE WALK

❶ Walk beside the village green to return to the road. The charming thatched cottage facing the green dates from the 14th

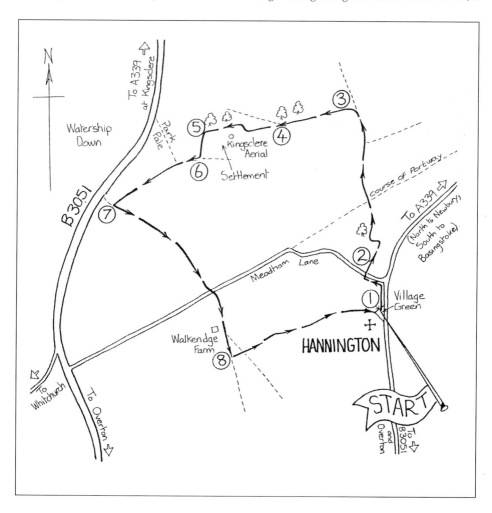

Looking north from the chalk escarpment near Hannington.

century. Turn left to walk through the village to the junction with Meadham Lane – the first lane on the left. Follow Meadham Lane to a bridleway sign on the right.

❷ Turn right through a gate and follow the path uphill with a hedge on the right to a gap opening into a field. The path swings left here for about 100 yards then turns right, to run beside a wood on the left and fields on the right. The path leaves the wood and drops down into a valley over the route of the Portway and climbs to join a white track. Follow the bridleway sign ahead down the white track. As the hedge on the left gives way to a wire fence look carefully for a stile on the left marked with footpath signs.

❸ Turn left over the stile and follow a narrow path along the edge of the down with a fence on your left. Now you enjoy magnificent views all the way. After running through a fringe of trees, and then a small pine wood, the path divides.

❹ Keep straight on at the division, maintaining your height, keeping the trees on your right and the fence on your left. Continue over a stile and follow a narrow path between bushes. The tall Kingsclere aerial is further up the field on the left.

PLACES of INTEREST

West of Hannington, on the other side of the B3051, is **Watership Down**, made famous by Richard Adams. This walk can easily be lengthened to include a ramble along one of the many footpaths crossing the down.

The path bears right for a few yards then left to continue, with the fence on the left and woods on the right, to a footpath sign on the left beside a stile.

❺ Turn left over the stile into a field. There is no clear path at this point but keep straight ahead up the field aiming for the right-hand edge of a wood. Here you pick up a good path. Humps in the field on your left mark the site of a former village. Follow the path round the wood, leaving it on your left, towards a metal gate and stile.

❻ Turn right just before the gate and stile and walk along the top of the field. The path descends past the ridge of Park Pale. Cross double stiles and bear a little left then right to resume your former heading, with a hedge on the left. Descend through fields for about ½ mile and reach a stile.

❼ Go over the stile to a crossing path and turn left to follow the path as it climbs gently uphill beside fields with a hedge on the right. Continue for about ¾ mile as the path becomes hedged on the left. Keep to the path as it drops downhill to Meadham Lane. Turn left for a few yards then turn right down a metalled farm road. Pass Walkeridge Farm on the right and continue ahead with a hedge on the left to walk down to a wooden gate.

❽ Go through the gate and turn immediately left to walk up the field. At the far side follow the sign ahead and continue for about ¾ mile to a small wooden gate on the right. Go through the gate and follow the path with a fence on the left. Cross the stile ahead, walk over the grass to cross another stile and follow the footpath sign beside trees on your right. The path curves right round a barn. Turn left to return to Hannington village green.

SHERFIELD ON LODDON

Length: 5 miles

Getting there: Sherfield on Loddon is about 4 miles north of Basingstoke. The village is now bypassed by the A33. Turn off the A33 following the sign for the village.

Parking: Drive over the crossroads in front of the post office and take the Bramley road (between two 40 mph signs). The car park is signed a few yards down the Bramley

Road on the left.

Map: OS Landranger 186 Aldershot & Guildford (GR 680580).

Sherfield on Loddon is an amazing village, a small part of medieval England that has survived to modern times. At first sight the village may appear quite ordinary as there are few old buildings. But the shape of the village can have changed little since Chaucer's day. The houses, often built on ancient sites, are scattered around a huge green, once a common and until recently home to a thriving community of cows, goats, horses, pigs, donkeys and geese. In 1972 a committee was formed to restore the green and now it is once more central to village life, a delightful place with sports fields, woods and open grassland enjoyed by everyone.

FOOD and DRINK

The village has two fine Inns, the White Hart (telephone: 01256 882280) and the Four Horseshoes (telephone: 01256 882296). Both offer excellent meals.

moated sites, and runs through small copses and woods once part of the ancient forest of Windsor and Eversley. The River Loddon runs through the meadows east of Sherfield on Loddon and we follow its course to return to the village.

There is a medieval 'feel' also about the surrounding countryside. This very pretty walk passes farms standing on

THE WALK

❶ Turn right from the car park to the crossroads and turn right again to pass the post office and the Four Horseshoes Inn

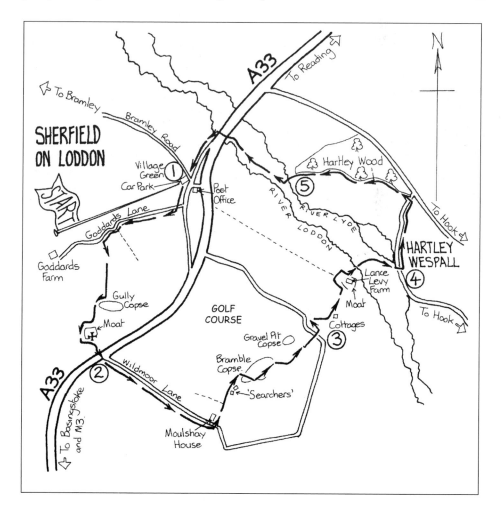

An attractive footbridge leads over the River Lyde near Hartley Wespall Mill.

on your left. Continue past the Old School House, still surmounted by its bell, and the village hall. Just past 'The Shop' turn right along Goddards Lane. Keep straight on past the no-through-road sign. Ignore a stile and footpath sign on the left and continue for about another 120 yards to a stile by a gate and track on the left. Turn left following the footpath sign and keep ahead beside the field with a fence on the right. Cross a stile and with a hedge on the right walk on to a wood, ancient Gully Copse. Turn right in front of the wood to go through a gate and follow a narrow path with a high hedge on your right. The path curves left beside the wood to a field. Bear a little left to walk beside the field. To your left runs an avenue of poplars planted in 1925 by Lord Gerald Wellesley, later 7th Duke of Wellington.

Bear right keeping the field on your right, then bear left to pass the high embankment of a moat. Brick foundations have been found on the island. Continue beside the embankment for about 200 yards to a stile on the left. Cross the stile and walk beside the churchyard to St Leonard's church. The church marks the site of an earlier Sherfield, possibly deserted after plague in the 14th century. Turn right down the church path through the lychgate to the A33.

❷ Cross the road and follow Wildmoor Lane ahead, for about ¾ mile. Just past Moulshay House turn left along a gravel track signed 'Searchers'. Beware mischievous gnomes in a hollow ash tree! Leave 'Searchers', originally built to house lorries fitted with searchlights during the Second

World War, on your right, to walk beside a meadow to the corner of Bramble Copse. The right-of-way that formerly crossed the beautiful medieval deer park has been diverted as the park is now, unfortunately, two golf courses. So turn right and follow the path with the copse on your left for about 150 yards. Then turn left following the footpath to walk through the copse. Leave the trees to keep straight on over the grass to enter Gravel Pit Copse over a bridge. After about 30 yards leave the main track and turn left along a narrower path which curves right, through the trees to a crossing track. Turn left to leave the copse and rejoin Wildmoor Lane.

❸ Turn left along the lane which curves right to a T-junction. Turn right and follow the lane (marked as bridleway). The lane curves left in front of some cottages and continues to a track on the left with Lance Levy Farm directly ahead. The farm is an ancient estate and originally stood within the moat east of the house. Turn left along the track to leave the farm on your right. The track swings right between farm buildings to a crosstrack. Turn right for a few yards then left along a wide hedge-lined track, passing a cottage on the left. Go through a gate and cross a narrow meadow. Go over a stile and continue over a brick bridge over the River Loddon. Walk over the next meadow, aiming for the nearest pylon, to a crosspath. Bear right here to walk between the River Loddon on your right and the River Lyde closer on your left, aiming for a metal gate at the far side of the field. Bear left over a stile to cross a footbridge over the Lyde to a lane.

PLACES of INTEREST

Stratfield Saye, the Duke of Wellington's country house, is just to the north with its splendid grounds and exhibition. Cafe. Telephone: 01256 882882. South West is **The Vyne**, one of Hampshire's most interesting great houses with an exquisite early 16th-century chapel. Tearooms. Telephone: 01256 881337. And **Silchester Roman Town** is fascinating! The museum and site, northwest of Sherfield, are open throughout the year. Telephone: 01734 700362.

---

❹ Turn left to follow the lane through Hartley Wespall for about ⅓ mile to a T-junction. Just before them, turn left past the bus shelter and take the footpath sign on the left to go through a belt of trees. The path turns right to run to the left of Hartley Wood. Ignore a stile into the wood on the right and follow the edge of the wood to go over a stile on its western corner.

❺ Keep ahead over a bridge across a stream. Then bear right, slanting to the left of a line of power cables to meet the bank of the Loddon just before a gate opening to the A33. Cross the road and follow the narrow path a little to your left which leads to a quiet road. Follow the road to return to Sherfield on Loddon, turning right down Bramley Road back to your car.

GREYWELL

Length: 5 miles

Getting there: Greywell is a small village 2 miles south of the M3 between Basingstoke and Fleet. Turn off the M3 along the A287 signed Odiham and take the right-hand lane to turn right almost immediately following the sign for Greywell along the Hook Road. Approaching along the A287 turn left for Greywell just before the joining lanes for the motorway.

Parking: Follow the Hook Road for a mile into Greywell village. Pass the Fox and Goose pub on the right and park by the roadside. Alternatively you may prefer to patronise the pub and turn right into the pub car park.

The proprietor is happy for you to use the car park while you walk provided you have a word with her first.

Map: OS Landranger 186 Aldershot & Guildford (GR 718514).

Greywell comes as a surprise. Not far away traffic thunders past on the motorway but this tiny old-world village remains remote and peaceful, surrounded by nature reserves exceptionally rich in wildlife. A single row of houses and cottages, many timber-framed, borders the village street overlooking the meadows sloping down to the River Whitewater. Closer to the river stands the little church built in the 12th

FOOD and DRINK

I can recommend the Fox and Goose for its excellent food and ales and warm hospitality. Telephone: 01256 702062.

century, with the marks of Crusaders' crosses on the doorway. Inside, the chancel screen dates from about 1500 and there is a loft above for the rood. From the church a path leads to an old half-timbered mill beside a pond fringed with rushes and yellow flag irises. But Greywell is not only beautiful – it is also famous! When the Basingstoke canal was completed in 1794 to link the market town via the Wey Navigation and the Thames with London, a tunnel was constructed from Greywell to carry the canal under Lord Tylney's land. In 1932 part of the tunnel collapsed and it is now home to the largest bat roost in Britain, designated a wildlife heritage site of world importance.

This walk starts from the tunnel's eastern entrance which was restored in 1976. The route follows the canal towpath over the River Whitewater to the impressive ruins of Odiham Castle (sometimes called King John's Castle). We continue beside the canal to North Warnborough, cross Swan Bridge to rejoin the canal briefly then take field paths to Greywell Moors, a nature reserve dedicated to the memory of an eminent botanist, Ted Wallace. A beautiful path leads over the reserve and beside the River Whitewater past the mill to return to Greywell.

The ruins of King John's Castle close to the towpath of the Basingstoke canal.

THE WALK

❶ Leaving the Fox and Goose pub on your left walk to the junction with Deptford Lane. Turn right for a few yards then follow the footpath sign on the left to cross the tunnel entrance and bear right to the canal towpath. Follow the towpath with the canal on your right. At first the water is clear, flowing over waving fronds of weed. After a barrier the water clouds but it is still popular with lively families of ducks, coots and moorhens. The canal crosses the River Whitewater and soon you will see the ruined keep of Odiham

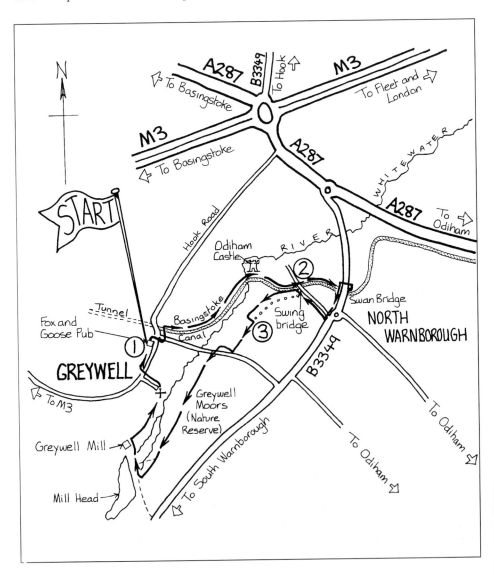

Castle over the grass on your left. This romantic ruin is all that remains of a castle built by King John in 1207. From here he rode out to set his seal on the Magna Carta at Runnymede. The canal curves a little right to a swing bridge.

❷ Cross the lane that leads over the swing bridge and continue beside the canal to a brick bridge. Go under the bridge then turn left up the steps to the pavement beside the B3349, opposite the Swan pub in North Warnborough. Cross the road and turn left over the bridge towards a traffic island. Before the island, turn right along The Street, an old part of the village with some thatched and jettied houses. Continue for about 100 yards then turn right down a lane signed 'Unsuitable for motors' which leads to the canal by the swing bridge. Turn left beside the canal, with the canal on your right, for about 200 yards to a stile on your left. Cross the stile and continue along the side of a field, a hedge on your left, past a stile to another stile on your left. Turn left over the stile and follow the hedged path ahead for a few yards to the point where it turns right at ❸.

❸ Continue along the hedged path to a lane. Turn right and follow the lane round a left hand bend past a pumping station to a gate and footpath sign on the left. Turn left to follow the path over Greywell Moors for about a mile. Chalk springs rising here to run through marshes to join the River Whitewater have created a fen with many rare plants including marsh helleborine, Dyers greenweed and pepper-saxifrage. After a gate the path divides.

PLACES of INTEREST

To find out more about the **Basingstoke Canal**, and see a reconstruction, visit the Basingstoke Visitor Canal Centre. The Centre is in Mytchett Place Road, Mytchett, Surrey. Telephone: 01252 370073. At **Basing House**, Old Basing, are the magnificent ruins of the Tudor palace besieged for two years by Cromwell's soldiers. Telephone: 01256 467294.

Keep ahead along the left-hand path through trees. The path curves right to a crosspath. Turn right to follow a glorious path through banks of flowers beside the watery expanse of the mill-head on your left. Bear left round the mill – the wheel and its workings are clearly visible – and follow the footpath sign pointing right to continue with the river on your right. Walk through the churchyard, past the church and turn left through double gates to take the church path to the road in Greywell. Turn right to return to your car.

OLD ALRESFORD

Length: 4½ miles

Getting there: Old Alresford lies beside the B3046 in the valley of the River Alre 2 miles north of its confluence with the River Itchen. The best approach is via the A31. Turn off the A31 for New Alresford, follow the B3046 through New Alresford and turn down Broad Street to cross the River Alre. Drive into Old Alresford.

Parking: Drive past the church and turn left just past the phone box on the left to face the Christy Memorial Hall. Turn left in front of the hall and leave your car in the car park on the right just past the building.

Map: OS Landranger 185 Winchester & Basingstoke (GR 587341).

Old Alresford is a village of quiet charm. The houses, some dating from the 17th and 18th centuries, overlook wide greens shaded by majestic trees. An earlier village was destroyed by fire and was rebuilt by Bishop de Lucy in the 12th century. He also built a causeway over the Alre to his New Market, now known as New Alresford. The causeway, crossed by the B3046 today, also served as a dam, creating Old Alresford Pond. Originally it provided power for corn and fulling mills and fish for the Bishop's table. Now it is a haven for wildlife. The beautiful church of St

FOOD and DRINK

The Globe on the Lake, just over the causeway in New Alresford, is an excellent pub, beautifully sited beside Old Alresford Pond. It serves interesting and imaginative food using local produce when possible. Telephone: 01962 732294.

Mary is mainly 18th century and is listed as a building 'of special architectural and historic interest'. Inside is an appealing memorial to Jane, the first wife of Admiral Lord Rodney who lived nearby in Old Alresford House There is also a memorial to Mary Sumner, the wife of Reverend George Sumner, appointed Rector in 1850. She founded the Mothers' Union, holding the first meetings in the rectory, now Old Alresford Place.

This superb walk follows an old drovers' track for almost 2 miles across Abbotstone Down to the site of the medieval village of Abbotstone. The outlines of streets and houses can still be traced. Paths then lead down into the valley of the Alre. We take a memorable stroll along the bank of this beautiful river past a 13th century fulling mill, before following the footway over Bishop de Lucy's causeway to return to Old Alresford.

THE WALK
❶ Turn right from the car park along the road with the green on your left. Across the grass a spring has been piped into a brook. Pass a footpath sign on the right and continue down the road to the children's playground on the corner.

❷ Take the lane on the right and after about 100 yards keep straight on along a wide grassy track, the ancient Ox Drove Way. The path sinks deep between high hedges, then rises to run through more open country giving views to the south over undulating fields and woods. Pass a footpath sign on the left and continue ahead for around ½ mile to pass a track on the left which leads down to Fobdown Farm. After running beneath tall trees the path swings a little left then right to follow the edge of a field, with hedges still on the right. Follow the path to a lane.

❸ Turn left into this quiet lane which runs across the site of Abbotstone medieval village. As in so many villages, the people of Abbotstone suffered from the Black Death in 1349 and 1350, but the final decline began during the 18th century when the introduction of machinery combined with poor wages led many agricultural workers to leave the land. The lane winds downhill bearing a little right into the wooded valley of the Alre. Pass Fobdown Farm on the left and continue past a lane leading to watercress beds on the right. The lane now rises a little as you follow it for another ¼ mile to a broad track on the right marked with a right-of-way sign.

PLACES of INTEREST

Mid-Hampshire's steam railway, the **Watercress Line** running between New Alresford and Alton, provides a wonderful day out for all the family. Telephone: 01962 733810.

Old Alresford House is open in August 2pm to 6pm, Wednesday to Sunday. Telephone: 01962 732843.

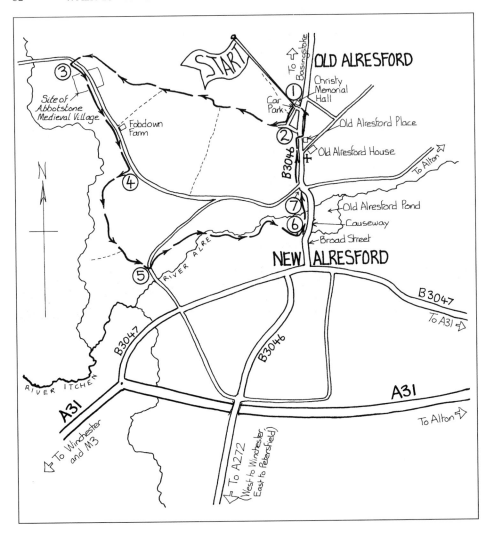

❹ Turn right and walk downhill to a crossing track. Turn left. The track becomes a pleasant grassy way running between trees and hedges and rises to meet a lane.

❺ Cross the lane, bear left for a few yards, then follow the footpath sign on the right to take a footpath which bears half-right away from the lane. There is a field on your left and a high hedge on your right. Keep ahead along a narrow path between trees. Leave the trees to continue past some houses on the right and later a stile on the left to walk downhill to the streamside. Turn right over a small brick bridge then turn left to walk between the stream and the Alre on your right. Turn right past

The 13th-century fulling mill on the River Alre.

a brick building to cross the Alre, then left to walk along the bank. The walk becomes really lovely with the river flowing serenely beside you. Look for a small headstone on the right of the path marking the grave of a much-loved dog, Hambone Jr, 'faithful friend of the 47th Infantry Regiment, 9th Division, US Army, May 1944'.

When you come to a road, cross over and continue along the bank following the sign for the fulling mill. Pass this delightful timber-framed house to join a lane and continue to a road.

❻ Turn left down the road past the Town Mill and keep straight on for Alre Mill with a stream on your right. Pass the watercress beds and keep ahead to a road junction.

❼ Walk over to the main road, the B3046, and follow the raised footpath to the left of the road into Old Alresford. Pass the church and continue along the footpath which now runs to the right of the main road. Turn left to cross the green by the phone box and return to your car.

CHAWTON

Length: 4 miles

Getting there: Chawton is 2 miles south of Alton. It is now bypassed by both the A31 and the A32. Turn for the village following the signs for Jane	Austen's House. **Parking:** In the public car park on the right opposite Jane Austen's House, just beyond the	car park for the Grey Friar Inn. **Map:** OS Landranger 186 Aldershot & Guildford (GR 709376).

'Everybody is acquainted with Chawton and speaks of it as a remarkably pretty village', wrote Jane Austen to her sister Cassandra, happily anticipating their move from lodgings into a home of their own, Chawton Cottage, in July 1809. Now called Jane Austen's House, the cottage, homely and comfortable in its attractive garden, is beautifully maintained and looks very much as she left it. Here she enjoyed a settled life once more and could return to her storytelling. By the window in the living room of the cottage you can see the small table at which she sat to revise her early novels and write the great novels of her maturity, *Mansfield Park, Emma* and *Persuasion*. And she would still recognise the village. In spite of the fame she has

FOOD and DRINK

Cassandra's Cup, opposite Jane Austen's House serves excellent coffee, lunches and teas. Telephone: 01420 83144.
I can also recommend the Grey Friar Inn for good home-cooking. Telephone: 01420 83841.

brought to this corner of Hampshire, Chawton remains unspoilt, a single street of timber-framed and early Georgian houses surrounded by the pleasant open countryside in which she walked and found inspiration for her novels.

The route of this walk follows Jane past Chawton House, the home of her rich brother Edward. Chawton Estate was part of his inheritance from wealthy relatives, the Knights, who had adopted him as a child. We continue in her footsteps to visit some clerical neighbours, the Benn family at Farringdon, another delightful old world village, before following the track of the former railway to return to Chawton.

THE WALK

❶ From the entrance to the car park turn left along the old road marked with a no-through-road sign. This was part of the A32 before the bypass was constructed, now it is a quiet lane overlooked by a row of ancient cruck cottages. They are named 'Pond Cottages', a reminder that in Jane's time there was a pond at the junction with the main Winchester to London road in front of her house. Parkland, dotted with fine trees, rises on your left. The large house set back from the road on the right was the rectory in 1809. The vicar was a bachelor, Mr Papillon, who in Mrs Knight's opinion was the perfect match for Jane. Much amused,

Jane wrote to Cassandra, 'she may depend upon it, I *will* marry Mr Papillon, whatever may be his reluctance or my own!' On the left a drive runs down to Edward's home, Chawton House, a grey Elizabethan mansion with a square porch and heavy mullioned windows. Jane spent many hours here amusing Edward's large family with stories in which, as a niece recalls, the people 'all had characters of their own'. Her mother and sister are buried beside the little church to the right of the drive.

❷ Continue straight ahead at the end of the road along a narrow path through the trees. Turn left over a stile then turn right to resume your former heading between fences with a hedge on your right. Cross the next stile and continue beside the hedge to go over another stile.

❸ A clear footpath now runs half-left diagonally up a field. Follow this to a wood. Take the track through the trees then keep ahead beside a field with a hedge on the right. You enter woods again to walk between magnificent pines, then down an avenue of yews.

❹ Go straight over a crosstrack, past a children's playground and turn immedi-

PLACES of INTEREST

Jane Austen's House is a private museum administered by the Jane Austen Memorial Trust. It is open all week from 1st April to 31st October. In November, December and March it opens Wednesday to Sunday, and in January and February on Saturday and Sunday only. Times: 11 am to 4.30 pm. Telephone: 01420 83262.

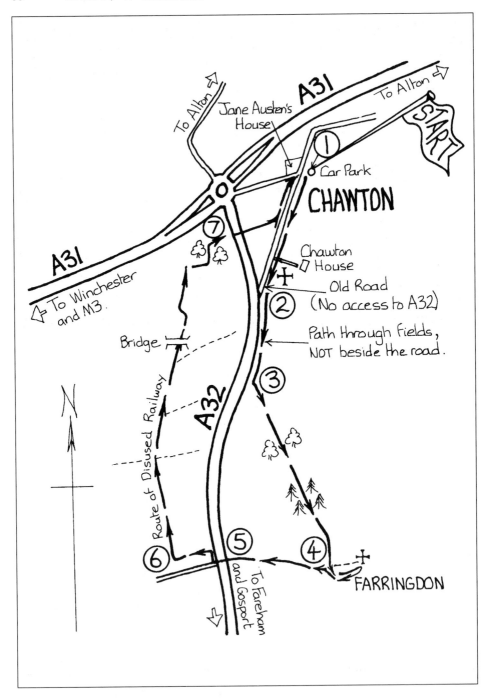

Jane Austen's house at Chawton.

ately left along a narrow path leading to gravel tracks in Farringdon village. Jane would turn left here to the rectory or right to the church. To see Farringdon's beautiful 13th century church, turn right for a few yards then left through the churchyard gate. The walk-through yew tree on the left is reputed to have stood there for 3,000 years! Retrace your steps to the crosstrack at ❹ and turn left to walk down to the A32.

❺ Cross the road and follow the narrow footpath running just to the right of the lane ahead. Climb a stile and follow the path, which runs past some metal buildings on the left. Continue along the edge of a field, trees on the left, to the track of the former railway, part of the Meon Valley line closed in 1955.

❻ Turn right to follow this tree-shaded way and keep ahead over all crosstracks. When the gravel track swings right keep ahead, still following the railway, under a bridge to a field. Bear left for a few yards, then right along the edge of the field for about ¼ mile. Turn right at the sign towards a small copse. Bear left to walk through the copse to cross a stile into a field.

❼ Turn right to walk down the field and over another stile to go down steps to the A32. Cross straight over, go up the steps, cross the stile and walk straight ahead beside a field, a hedge on your right. Over the next stile a narrow path leads to a close in Chawton. Walk through the close to rejoin the quiet lane (the former A32) you followed at the start of the walk. Turn left to return to the car park.

SELBORNE

Length: 4½ miles

Getting there: Selborne lies beside the B3006 which links the A31 at Alton with the A325 at Greatham. Follow the brown signs for 'Gilbert White's House'.

Parking: Drive into the village and turn into the public car park behind the Selborne Arms pub.

Map: OS Landranger 186 Aldershot & Guildford (GR 742335).

In 1789, an obscure country clergyman published a book about a quiet Hampshire village. Since then it has never been out of print. In *The Natural History and Antiquities of Selborne* the Rev Gilbert White lovingly observed and meticulously recorded the natural world surrounding 'The Wakes', his home in the High Street of this attractive village. He made several original discoveries including the harvest mouse (now returned to Selborne after an absence of 25 years!) and was the first to recognise the importance of earthworms in improving the texture of soil. But he is no mere observer, his most endearing quality is the delight he takes in all he sees. He

FOOD and DRINK

Selborne has two excellent pubs both serving hot and cold food all day: The Queen's Hotel (telephone: 01420 511454) and The Selborne Arms (telephone: 01420 511247). Bush House is a licensed restaurant, (telephone: 01420 511339). 'The Wakes' has a Tea Parlour where you can sample 18th century recipes.

path leading uphill on the left. This twisting and turning path makes the climb wonderfully easy and you are rewarded with really dramatic views. Continue past a metal bench to the top of the hill and bear right to a seat on your left. Just past the seat is a sarsen stone on your right. The stone was placed there by Gilbert White who called it his 'wishing stone'.

mere observer, his most endearing quality is the delight he takes in all he sees. He had a beautiful world to explore: beyond his garden rose a steep beech-clad hill called in Hampshire terms a Hanger, and north of the church opposite his home he could wander through the meadows of a delightful valley or take woodland paths along the hillsides which retained their Saxon names of the Long and Short Lythes. Today very little has changed. Selborne is remarkably unspoilt by fame and the countryside is still as lovely.

This is a walk in Gilbert White's footsteps. We take the Zig-Zag path he cut to the top of the Hanger to enjoy a marvellous view over the village and surrounding countryside. A walk through the woods and along the foot of the Hanger leads back to the village. From the church we follow his paths through the valley to the site of an old priory, now a farm, and return beneath the magnificent beech trees of Dorton Woods.

THE WALK

❶ Return to the entrance to the car park and turn right following the footpath sign for the Zig-Zag path and the Hanger. The path leads to a gate at the foot of the hill. Go through the gate and take the Zig-Zag

❷ Navigate carefully here! Continue past the seat on your left and the stone on your right along the path ahead close to the side of the Hanger. (Disregard the path on your left which leads behind the seat to Selborne Common. This runs parallel with your path for about 30 yards.) Follow the path under the magnificent beech trees which clothe the steep sides of the Hanger. Gilbert White considered beeches to be 'the most lovely of all forest trees'. After about ¼ mile you will see a metal bench by a downhill path on the right. Pause here for another fine view of Selborne before resuming your way through the woods, keeping to the main path as it descends to meet a joining path on the right at the foot of the hillside.

PLACES of INTEREST

The Wakes is a 16th century house, with later additions. The garden is almost as it was in Gilbert White's time with many of the features he mentions in his letters. The house also contains **The Oates Museum** commemorating Frank Oates' journeys to South America and South Africa and Captain Lawrence Oates who accompanied Scott to the South Pole. Open: 11 am to 5 pm daily mid-March to Christmas. Weekends only the rest of the year. Telephone: 01420 511275.

View of the village from Selborne Hanger.

3 Turn right with trees on your right and a hedge fringing meadows on your left. The path runs a little downhill and curves slightly left to meet a lane, Gracious Street, opposite Grange Farm. To the left of the lane is the tiny Oakhanger stream. Turn right to follow Gracious Street to Selborne High Street, cross over and take the footpath ahead leading to the church. You cross The Plestor – the name means 'play place' and it was once the site for fairs and markets. On the left you pass the old vicarage where Gilbert White was born in 1720. Our way is straight ahead through the gate signed 'Footpath to the Short and Long Lythe' but make a detour to visit the church, which dates from the 12th century and has beautiful windows commemorating Gilbert White. His grave is signposted north of the church.

Gilbert White's house.

❹ Follow the footpath across the church-yard and through a gate. A lovely valley opens before you. Follow the path down Church Meadow, cross a bridge and continue through two gates along the foot of the Short and Long Lythes to go through a third gate opening into Coombe Meadow.

❺ Disregard the green arrow Hangers Way sign and bear a little right diagonally across the meadow, keeping a lake and a stream over the grass on your right, passing a small lake on your left, towards Coombe Wood. Cross the stile into the wood and take the right-hand path at the division. At the end of the wood cross the stile and keep ahead with the wood on your left to cross another stile to a fenced path. Ignore

the stile ahead and turn right down the path. Go through the gate into Priory Farm and bear right round the buildings to a metalled track. Bear right again for a few yards and when the track swings left, keep straight on along a gravelled track to pass a bungalow on the left. Go through a gate and follow the path beside a meadow to go through another gate into Dorton Woods. The woodland path you now follow runs for over a mile to a metalled lane. Walk up the lane, which sinks deep beneath tree roots at one point revealing the white malmstone from which so many of the local houses are built. When you reach Selborne High Street turn left to return to your car.

CHERITON

Length: 4½ miles

Getting there: Cheriton lies in the valley of the River Itchen 7 miles east of Winchester beside the B3046. You can approach from the south by turning for the village off the A272 or from the north by fol-

lowing the B3046 from New Alresford.

Parking: Drive into the village and turn east off the main road by the war memorial into a minor road where there is good

roadside parking.

Map: OS Landranger 185 Winchester & Basingstoke (GR 583286).

If you imagine a miniature and more homely version of Venice then you will be able to picture Cheriton! For this old-world village, close to the source of the Itchen, is threaded by a network of sparkling streams flowing through green lawns and under tiny bridges. Many of the houses and cottages are thatched and date from the 16th century. Gardens overflow with flowers and gates open onto stream-side footpaths, happy playgrounds for children and ducks. The church of St Michael and All Angels, built during the 13th century, stands on a hill in the centre

---

FOOD and DRINK

The Flower Pots Inn has its own brewery and besides excellent ales it provides good home-cooked food. Telephone: 01962 771318.

---

of the village. The stained glass windows in the nave were installed by Mrs Phipps Egerton in memory of four nephews killed in the First World War. Each of the four windows depicts a knight personifying duty, courage, loyalty and honour and the faces are those of her nephews.

Thoughts of war seem far removed from Cheriton, slumbering peacefully in its river valley, but in 1644 the most decisive battle of the Civil War was fought on the high downs east of the village. This walk climbs to the site of the battle, little changed since Cavalier faced Roundhead across the fields. A beautiful path beneath the beech trees of Cheriton Wood leads to a track over the battlefield and the downs beyond. After a steep descent into the Itchen valley, field paths beside the river take us back to Cheriton.

THE WALK

❶ Turn left along the minor road in Cheriton with the green on your right towards a 30 mph sign. Just past the sign you will see a small brick bridge on the left and beyond it a large overhead sign for Freeman's Yard. Turn left to follow the lane running past the entrance to Freeman's Yard with a stream on your right. Continue for about 50 yards until just past a house named 'Martyrwell' you come to a footpath on the left.

❷ Turn left over a low wooden barrier and follow the narrow path between a flint wall on the left (later a fence) and a fence on the right. The path rises gently uphill to continue between hedges then follows the side of a meadow with a hedge on the right. You now have a splendid view of the 1644 battlefield. Ahead of you lies a shallow valley shaped like a horseshoe with the dark line of Cheriton Wood forming the eastern rim. The Parliamentary troops established their positions along the southern ridge of the horseshoe facing troops loyal to the King who had assembled on the northern slopes. Under the expert leadership of Sir William Waller, who commanded an army of 10,000 men and an artillery train of 16 cannon (greatly outnumbering his opponents), the Roundheads were the victors. This battle turned the tide in favour of Parliament.

❸ At the top of the meadow cross the stile and turn right with a field on your left and a hedge on your right. The path curves left beside the field with a hedge still on the right. You are now following the southern ridge crossing Lamborough Fields where the Roundhead army camped the night before the battle. They chose their situation wisely as there are wide views south over the Hinton Ampner valley as well as north over the downs. Cross the next stile and keep ahead down

---

PLACES of INTEREST

Hinton Ampner House and Gardens (National Trust) are open at varying times from Easter to September. Telephone: 01962 771305.

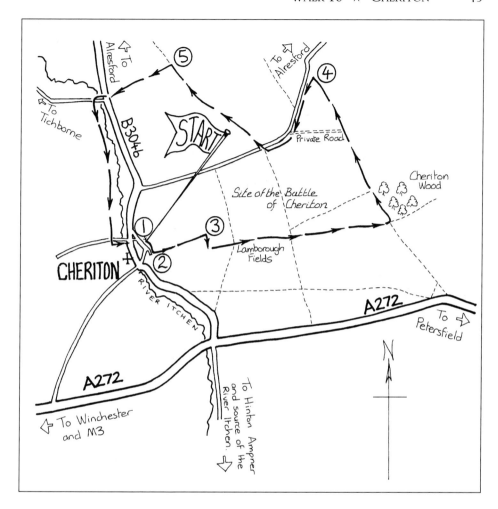

a wide green path to a crosspath. Go straight over and continue to another crosspath. Cross over and go through a small wooden gate to follow a narrow path beside a field along the top of the ridge with a hedge on your right. In a little under ½ mile you come to Cheriton Wood. Go through a wooden gate and a few yards further on turn left to follow the path just inside the wood. The path leaves the wood to descend into the valley and mount the northern ridge. Pass a track on the left signed 'Private Road' and continue for about ¼ mile to meet a lane.

❹ Turn left down the lane. Ignore a footpath sign and keep to the lane as it curves right to bring you to a track on the right with a footpath sign. Turn right and follow the track for about ¾ mile. When you are about half-way you pass a joining path on the left. Keep ahead a little uphill to the

A branch of the Itchen flows lazily through the water meadows between carpets of watercress near Cheriton.

next path on the left, indicated by a small wooden post marked with arrows on the right.

❺ Turn left to walk down this attractive green path leading directly downhill. You can see the rooftops of Cheriton village in the valley. Walk over the main road, the B3046, and follow the lane ahead signed for Tichborne, crossing small bridges over the Itchen. At this point the river is divided into several streams running lazily through the meadows between mats of watercress. Pass the first of the Cheriton Mill buildings then turn left following the footpath sign along the metalled drive between the buildings. Go through a gate and continue over lawns past a house on the right. Cross a stile and keep ahead along the lower edge of a meadow with the river running behind a screen of tall trees on your left. Continue over more stiles and fields for about ¾ mile to meet a lane in Cheriton. Turn left to walk down to the B3046. Cross over and follow the minor road ahead which curves right to take you back to your car.

MEONSTOKE

Length: 5½ miles

Getting there: Meonstoke is about 12 miles north of Fareham beside the A32.	Parking: Approaching from the south turn right for the village and park almost immediately by the wall on the left.	Map: OS Landranger 185 Winchester & Basingstoke (GR 612201).

After the last of the Roman Legions had left Britain around AD 410, a Jutish tribe, the Meonwaras, sailed up the Solent and established settlements in the beautiful Hampshire river valley to which they gave their name. Meonstoke, on the east bank of the river, was the tribal centre. Today all is peace. The river flows through green lawns surrounding a 13th century church. Up the hill creeper-covered Georgian houses line a superb High Street which runs parallel with the main road but belongs to a different world. Half-way down, the houses give way to a group of thatched barns! But in the past conflict between the Meonwaras and their Romano-British neighbours in Exton on the other side of the Meon led to an enmity which lasted for hundreds of years. The bridge across the river linking the two

FOOD and DRINK

The Buck's Head serves good food and ales and is beautifully situated beside the river. Telephone: 01489 877313.

villages was not built until 1805!

Although the Meonwaras gave their name to the village, they were relative newcomers. Two thousand years earlier the peoples of the Bronze Age had buried their dead in the numerous tumuli that dot the hillsides. Later, Iron Age tribes built a fort on top of an outlying spur of the South Downs, now called Old Winchester Hill, just east of the village.

The magnificent view from the Iron Age fort ringing Old Winchester Hill is the highlight of this splendid walk. Most of the ascent is gradual along pleasant footpaths. The return route is quick and easy along a track which crosses the disused railway and footbridges over the

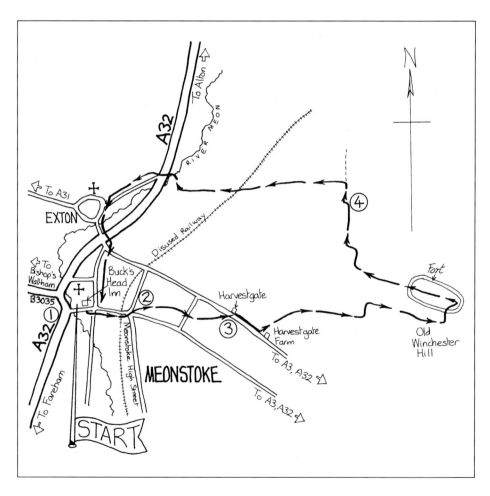

On top of Old Winchester Hill.

Meon to visit Exton, another beautiful village. A short walk through Meonstoke brings you back to your car.

THE WALK

❶ Walk up the road leaving the front of the Buck's Head pub on your left. At the top of the road, in front of a grassy triangle, bear left for a few yards then turn right along Pound Lane. Follow the lane past Pound Cottages, cross the bridge over the disused railway and continue downhill for about 50 yards to a crossroads. Bear left to a stile and footpath sign on the right.

❷ Climb the stile and follow the path straight ahead across a field to go over another stile. Keep ahead with a hedge close on the right, turning left at the corner of the field to a stile on the right.

Cross the stile to a lane. Over the lane another stile leads to a path straight ahead. Continue with a hedge on your right to cross a stile and now the path runs beside a meadow. After the next stile the path runs half-left diagonally over a field towards a house, Harvestgate. In front of the house you come to a lane.

❸ Turn right for about 200 yards to a track on the left just before Harvestgate

---

PLACES of INTEREST

Bishops Waltham is a few miles west of Meonstoke. The impressive remains of the 12th century palace of the Bishops of Winchester well repay a visit. Open daily April to September from 10 am to 1 pm, 2 pm to 6 pm. Telephone: 01489 892460.

Farm. Turn left for a few yards along the asphalt drive and when the drive turns right towards the house keep straight on along a wide hedged way. Over the fields a little to your right you will see Old Winchester Hill. The track curves in the direction of the hill then climbs gently towards the hill's right shoulder. When you come to a crossing track in front of a hedge turn left. After about 150 yards turn right following the path with the hedge still on your right. Keep to the path as it runs beside a small wood to a gate and Information Board on the left. Turn left through the gate to make the final steep but short climb up Old Winchester Hill. Near the top go through a small gate in front of the hill fort embankment and bear right. Keep to the main path which soon curves left to cross the top of the hill. This is a wonderful place with spectacular views in all directions. Looking south you can see over the Solent to the hills of the Isle of Wight.

Pass the trig point and orientation table on the left and follow the path through a gap in the western embankment. Continue downhill to go through a gate and walk through a rather mysterious wood. Further downhill turn right following a sign. Keep to the path as it bears left for about 30 yards then curves right. Continue down the side of a field with a belt of trees on your left, past a post with yellow arrow footpath signs. Keep straight on along the green track for about ¼ mile to another post on the left marked with footpath signs.

❹ Turn left at this second post through the trees to a track. Turn right to follow it for about 150 yards to a wide track on the left. Turn left and follow the track heading west for about ¾ mile. Cross the railway embankment by wooden steps and keep ahead with the stream on you left as the path narrows to run between hedges to a crosstrack. Turn right along a path which curves left to cross footbridges over the Meon to the main road, A32. Cross straight over and follow the lane ahead into Exton. At the junction bear left. Pass the Shoe pub and turn left over the Meon bridge to the A32. Cross and walk up Stocks Lane. At the top turn right and continue past a turning on the right to the grassy triangle. If you have time, make a short detour here and keep straight on to see Meonstoke's High Street. Retrace your steps to the triangle and walk down to your car.

BURITON

Length: 4½ miles

Getting there: Buriton is a mile east of the A3 about 3 miles south of Petersfield. Approaching from Petersfield turn left following the Buriton sign. Approaching from the south	turn left for Petersfield to go under the A3 then follow the Buriton signs. **Parking:** Drive through the village and park on the far side	of the pond in front of the church. **Map:** OS Landranger 197 Chichester & the South Downs (GR 739200).

Buriton is one of Hampshire's most attractive villages. It is beautifully situated in a secluded valley sheltered by the steep tree-covered slopes of the northern escarpment of the South Downs. The narrow High Street, lined with houses and cottages built of local cream-coloured malmstone, runs down to a pond complete with tribes of hungry ducks. The Norman church of St Mary stands on a slight rise overlooking the water. Next to the church is the Manor House which was rebuilt in the 18th century by the father of Edward Gibbon, the historian. Gibbon wrote a good deal of his book *The Decline and Fall of the Roman Empire* in the Manor in what is now called 'The Gibbon Room'. Pond, church and manor combine to make an idyllic scene and nicely sited waterside seats provide the perfect place to relax and enjoy it all!

Everyone will enjoy this easy walk through some of Hampshire's finest countryside. Much of the route follows paths in the more remote southern half of the Queen Elizabeth Country Park, the Queen Elizabeth Forest. Magnificent beech woods clothe the steep hillsides and there are splendid downland views. Wildlife includes dainty roe deer and among the great variety of wild flowers are twelve species of orchid. The Park is crossed by a labyrinth of paths and for ease of navigation as well as scenic value I have followed parts of the three long distance footpaths which run through the Forest, the South Downs Way, the Hangers Way and the Staunton Way. These are indicated in the walk directions.

THE WALK

❶ From the parking area walk round the pond leaving the church on your right. Bear left following the Hangers Way sign with the rectory on the right and the pond on the left along South Lane. Originally this narrow asphalt road had the much more interesting name of Toads Alley! You pass an attractive thatched malmstone

house on the left and then the way becomes gravelled as it runs under a railway bridge and begins to wind uphill through beech and chestnut woods. Keep to the main path, ignoring all joining paths on the left, to leave the trees in front of a road junction at Halls Hill car park.

❷ The road directly in front of you leads to Dean Barn. Turn right to cross another road to the car park. Leave the Halls Hill sign on your left. Continue past the stile and Hangers Way sign also on your left and keep straight ahead, following the sign for the South Downs Way through a gate. The track climbs beside the meadow to the edge of the tree-covered slope of War Down. Then the track bears left to run beside the woods, climbing gently and giving beautiful views over the valley and the wooded hillsides beyond. Pass a joining track on the right and shortly afterwards the way divides. Follow the right-hand track signed South Downs Way Walkers. Keep to the main path as it drops a little downhill past a barbecue area on the left at Benhams Bushes. Continue

PLACES of INTEREST

The Queen Elizabeth Country Park covers more than 1,000 acres of dramatic forest and downland scenery. There are facilities for a wide range of activities and trails for walkers, horse riders and cyclists. All information is available in the Visitor Centre and refreshments in the Coach House Cafe. An underpass leads to Butser Down, and **Butser Ancient Farm**, a reconstruction of an Iron Age settlement. The park is open throughout the year. For Centre opening times telephone: 01705 595040.

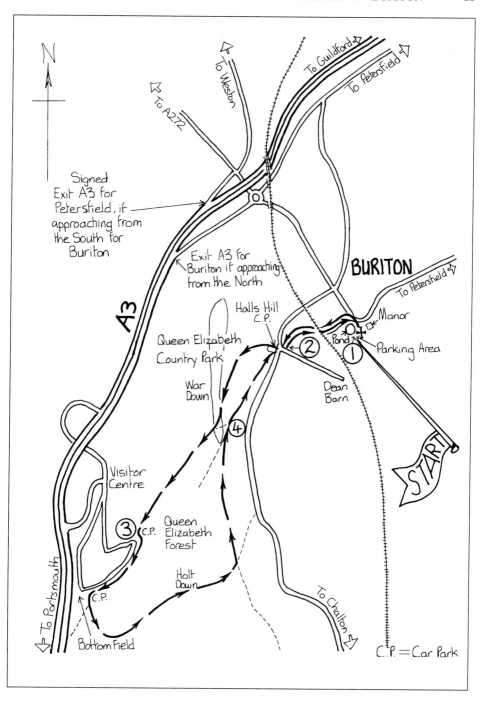

Halls Hill.

downhill to pass a wooden Forestry Commission barrier and another barbecue area also known as Benhams Bushes. Walk over a car park to the corner of a road.

❸ Bear left for about 100 yards then continue in the same direction along the footpath to the left of the road signed Hangers Way. This leads down to a car park near Bottom Field. Pass the car park on your right and walk over the grass to a crosstrack. Turn left following the Staunton Way sign which you will see a few yards away on your right. The track climbs to a division. Take the left-hand path which climbs gently through pine woods then curves left through open areas to give more lovely views. Keep to the main path over all crosstracks as it curves left round the side of Holt Down. The track begins to drop downhill and after about 100 yards a crosspath slants across your way. Take the first track on the left,

uphill, unsigned at this point. After a few yards you pass a small post on the left signed Hangers Way. The path becomes grassy and really beautiful now as it levels to run beneath the beech trees with a spectacular drop into the valley on the right. Keep to the main path until you come to a finger post on the right indicating the Hangers Way to left and right. A narrow earth path runs downhill from the post on the right. This is an alternative route of the Hangers Way and is also part of the Staunton Way.

❹ Turn right to follow the narrow path downhill. Go through a gate and follow the meadow path ahead with trees on your left to go through another gate. The path now leads across the meadow over two stiles to the car park at Halls Hill. Turn right, then left to retrace your steps along your former path back to Buriton and your car.

HAMBLEDON

Length: 3 miles

Getting there: Hambledon lies in south-east Hampshire about 6 miles north of Portsmouth between the A32 and the A3. Follow the B2150 which turns west off the A3 at Waterlooville signed for Denmead. Drive through Denmead following the signs for Hambledon.

Parking: Drive past the Hambledon village sign to a fork. The main village street is to the right but it is usually difficult to find parking space so continue along the left hand road, the B2150, for about 50 yards where there is room to park on the left.

Map: OS Landranger 196 The Solent & Isle of Wight (GR 642149).

Hambledon is an old-world village tucked so snugly in a wooded fold of the downs that it looks as if it has grown there! In the past the village prospered, holding two fairs a year in addition to a weekly market. A shop at the foot of Church Lane still bears the sign 'The People's Market'. Letters patent for holding the markets were stamped 'Broad-Half-Penny', the toll paid to the Lord of the Manor for setting up a booth. Today the toll name is inseparably linked with the down east of the village, the first home of Hambledon Cricket Club which was formed about 1750 and rapidly became the accepted authority.

All the houses are charming, many concealing half-timbered walls behind the rounded bow windows and pedimented doorways of Georgian days. The street up to the church is particularly attractive with its old cobbled pavements and colourful gardens. The church of St Peter and St Paul was built around a little Saxon church which still forms part of the nave.

This is a very rewarding walk. We climb the hillside south of the village, Speltham Down, to follow footpaths offering beautiful views before descending to cross the valley. The route then leads up the hill north of the village to return through ancient oak and beech woods.

THE WALK

❶ From the parking area walk down the road to the Y-junction and turn left along the main village street. You might like to make a detour to see Church Lane on your left. Retrace your steps to the main street. Across the road a lane leads right past the side of the George Hotel. Follow this lane uphill to a National Trust sign on the right by the footpaths at the approach to Speltham Down.

❷ Turn right through an iron gate and walk straight ahead along the foot of the down. Continue through a wooden gate for about ¼ mile to a second wooden gate.

❸ Go through the gate and turn left to follow the steps up the hillside. As you near the top the path runs through a belt of trees to a stile. Cross the stile and keep ahead along a narrow path over a field to a crosspath in front of another belt of woodland. Turn right and continue with the trees on your left. Leave the field to descend to a lane on the left.

❹ Cross the lane and go through an iron gate to follow the wide path ahead with trees on the left. Continue beside a field with the trees now on your right. Follow the path which leads through trees down to the B2150.

❺ Turn right beside the road – there is a grassy verge – for about 100 yards. Look carefully for a footpath sign on the left. Two paths are indicated. Go through a gate, following the sign indicating a narrow path leading half-right diagonally down the field to leave a pylon on the left. Cross a plank bridge to the right of some fencing and walk up a small field to cross a stile into a lane. Go over the lane and cross the stile on the other side. Walk up the meadow ahead, cross double stiles, and continue uphill to cross a stile leading into a wood, intriguingly named 'Madam's Copse'. (Ignore the crosspath in front of the stile.)

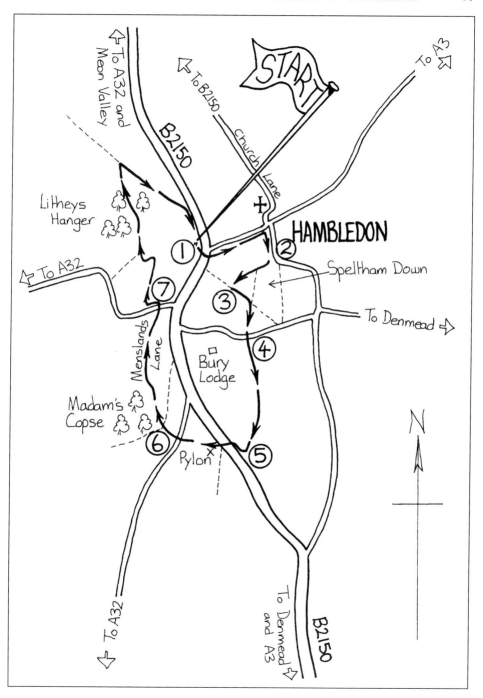

Hambledon

❻ Follow the woodland path and continue through a more open area. You are now high on the down and over to your right you will see a large house on the hillside. This is Bury Lodge, built close to the site of a Roman villa. The path now runs through more attractive woodland. Past an iron gate you meet a crosstrack called 'Menslands Lane'. Bear right along the track which becomes metalled as it traces the hillside with trees on the left. Continue past a footpath sign on the right to a lane.

❼ Turn left up the lane for about 40 yards to a footpath sign on the right. Turn right along a sunken track, then cross a stile to walk beside a field past a half-timbered barn. Cross the next stile and continue with a fence on the left and a hedge on the right to a crosstrack. Turn left uphill, then turn right over a stile and continue along the hillside to go over a stile into the woods of Litheys Hanger. The path bears a little right with deep pits on either side. Keep ahead over a crosstrack and follow the path to another crosstrack in front of a stile. A well-worn path leads right downhill forming a short-cut to the path we follow later but as it is not marked as a right-of-way you may prefer to take a longer way round. Cross the stile and another stile a few yards further on your right, and continue through a belt of trees along the top of a field for about 100 yards. Now turn acutely back (look for a green arrow on a tree on the right) and walk half-right down the field to a stile in the left-hand corner. Cross this and follow the woodland path over a stile downhill. The path curves left to the B2150. Turn right to your car.

An attractive barn raised on staddle stones in a meadow near Hambledon.

TITCHFIELD

Length: 5 miles

Getting there: Titchfield is a large village between Southampton and Fareham, lying in the Meon valley just south of the A27. Turn off the A27 following the sign 'Titchfield Village only'. Drive down Southampton Hill past the short stay car park on the right (limited to three hours and Titchfield is too good to rush!). Bear left at the foot of the hill signed 'Funtley' and follow the road round to the right. Turn left into Mill Street marked with a no-through-road sign. A few yards down the road you will see the Community Centre on the left. Turn left and park behind the Centre. (There is no access to Mill Street from the A27.)

Parking: As indicated above in the long-stay car park.

Map: OS Landranger 196 The Solent & Isle of Wight (GR 541061).

Discover Titchfield and enter a different world! This charming village only seconds away from the A27 is an oasis of calm surrounded by meadows and woods. The wide market place with its old coaching inns is approached by narrow streets lined with homely houses, some half-timbered and jettied, others dating from the 18th century with rounded bow windows and pillared doorways. A more peaceful scene

FOOD and DRINK

Titchfield has excellent inns and a bakery. The Bugle Hotel, a 17th-century coaching inn serves very good fare, with seafood a speciality. Telephone: 01329 841888.

would be hard to imagine but once the village, sited on the Meon estuary, was a busy port. Every year the villagers remember the fateful year 1611 when their landlord, the third Earl of Southampton, built a sea wall and one-way tidal flaps across the mouth of the Meon and put an end to their trade. A day-long carnival is held culminating in the lighting of a huge bonfire. To compensate, the third Earl constructed a canal from the village to the coast. As a navigable channel the canal was a failure but today the towpath provides a wonderful walk.

You follow the path beside the canal for almost 3 miles to reach the Solent at the Meon Shore. From there you have a splendid view over the Solent to the Isle of Wight. If you would like to see the attractive harbour at Hill Head you could make an optional detour here heading east along the coast. This will add an extra mile. The route of the walk heads west then turns inland to take field paths back to Titchfield.

THE WALK

❶ Do not return to the car park entrance. Take the footpath to the left of the Titchfield Community Association Youth Centre and follow this to cross the foot of Southampton Hill and walk down Titchfield High Street. Turn left along Church Street to St Peter's church. This welcoming church dates from the late 7th century and has a splendid Anglo-Saxon porch. The

Southampton chapel houses a magnificent monument erected by the second Earl in memory of his parents. Leave the church on your left and walk beside a wall on your right to cross a small bridge over the canal.

❷ Turn right to walk beside the canal which flows through the water meadows between carpets of white-flowered cress and thick stands of yellow flag irises and rushes. Cross a lane and continue through all gates, keeping to the towpath. As the canal-side path becomes grassy and hedged there are fine views over the drained estuary of the Meon on the left, now the Titchfield Haven Nature Reserve. This freshwater marsh includes wet meadows, dense reed beds and lagoons providing homes for a great variety of wildlife.

❸ Pass a footpath sign by a gate on the right (this marks the turn on our return route) and continue for a little under ½ mile past a footpath sign on the left. You are now close to the original sea lock at the mouth of the canal which has recently been restored. Pass the information board on your right and turn left over a stile just

PLACES of INTEREST

The ruins of **Titchfield Abbey** which the First Earl of Southampton bought and rebuilt as Place House, are open free of charge. Although Place House is now also a ruin, the magnificent gatehouse is well worth a visit. The third Earl was Shakespeare's patron and it is possible Shakespeare spent some time with the Earl at Place House. Open 10 am to 1 pm, 2 pm to 6 pm daily, Good Friday to September. Telephone: 01329 643016.

Titchfield Haven Nature Reserve and Visitor Centre are passed on the walk. Permits are required to visit the hides. Telephone: 01329 662145 or 01705 520213.

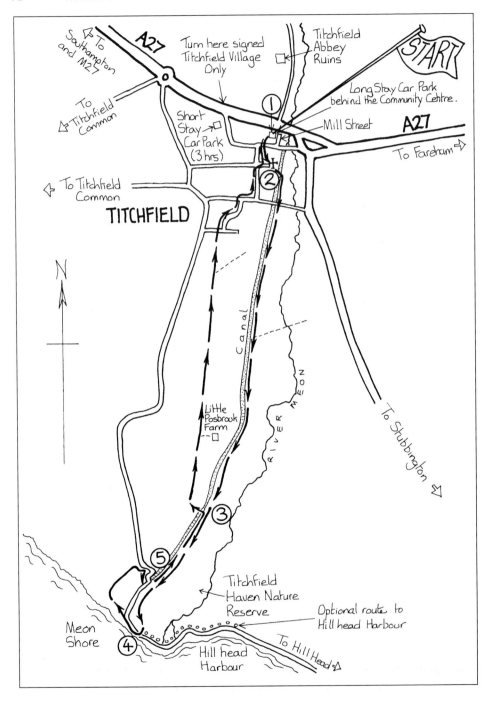

The Titchfield canal.

before the road. After a few yards the path bears right beneath trees then continues through reed beds past the sign for the Reserve Visitor Centre. Turn right through a small wooden gate and cross the road to the Meon Shore. (Turn left here for the optional walk to Hill Head harbour, then retrace your steps.)

❹ To continue the walk, turn right along the road. When the road curves right keep straight on between the beach chalets. Past the final chalet turn right up the bank to join a gravel track and walk up to the road. Turn right and follow the road as it bears left over the sea lock.

❺ Leave the road and turn left along our former path. Retrace your steps to the footpath on the left at ❸. Turn left over a

brick bridge, continue for about 100 yards then bear right as the sign directs to follow a path over the fields. You pass thatched Little Posbrook Farm in a dip on the right. Two trees stand either side of the drive, one commemorates the 50th anniversary of D-Day and the other of VE day. After passing a bungalow on the right the track curves right. Keep straight on beside a field, a hedge on the right. Keep ahead over stiles and fields to a road in front of houses at the approach to Titchfield. Cross the road and continue to the left of a high boarded fence with trees on your left. Cross a road and keep ahead along the pavement to the foot of Lower Bellfield Road. Turn right down Coach Hill, then left along South Street leading to the High Street. Walk down the High Street and follow the footpath to return to your car.

ACKNOWLEDGEMENTS

As always I am grateful to the staff of Southampton and Totton libraries for their assistance in providing me with books and helping me with my research. I would also like to thank all the people who helped me on my way especially the ladies in Titchfield church who provided hot coffee on a cold day! The staff in the post office in Sherfield on Loddon gave me much helpful information about their village and I received a most generous response to my request for information at the Queen Elizabeth Country Park. I am grateful for the never-failing interest and support of all my friends particularly Mary Chambers. Writing this book would not have been possible without the companionship of my husband Mike whose many duties included taking the photographs, performing miracles with map and compass and recording each walk on tape. Finally I would like to thank all my friends at Countryside Books for their advice and encouragement which has made writing this book such a pleasure.